THE CHILD IN THE MIDDLE

DELORIS CALHOUN-WRIGHT

ISBN: 9798251693645

Edited and Published by Educational Writing Services

Designed by Jennifer Carbuto Designs

DEDICATION

I dedicate this book to my beloved grandchildren, Kaleb Chambers, Reign Friday, and Cayden Foster, as a legacy of love, wisdom, and hope. May they grow up witnessing the power of co-parenting, kindness, and unwavering commitment to their well-being.

To my caring mother, Mary L. George, thank you for always reminding me to pray and never give up, and for instilling in me the foundation of love and peace.

Lastly, through these pages, I hope to provide guidance and encouragement for parents navigating the path of co-parenting, so that future generations can thrive in homes filled with respect, stability, and love. May this book serve as a reminder of the love and dedication that can surround and grow within each of us. And for those who may not always feel supported by love and dedication, may these pages offer encouragement, hope, and guidance. Let us embark on this journey together with open hearts and a shared goal of raising happy, resilient children in a world where love can rise above every difference.

ACKNOWLEDGEMENTS

Giving all glory to God, Heavenly Father, I come before You with a heart filled with gratitude. Before I thank anyone else, I must first thank you, Lord, for allowing me to write this book. Before I was even formed in my mother's womb, You knew who I was going to be, and You ordered this moment for me to walk in my purpose (Jeremiah 1:5). God, You get all the glory and praise. It was Your vision that led me, Your strength that sustained me, and Your courage that carried me through. Without You, this book would not have been possible. Thank You for being my guide, my source, my strength, and my inspiration. May this book serve Your will and touch the hearts You intend to reach.

To my support system, no journey is ever taken alone, and this book is no exception. As I transition into a new focus and season of purpose, I carry with me the lessons, strength, and encouragement that have helped shape both my path and this work.

I am deeply grateful for those who have supported, guided, and inspired me along the way. I would like to extend my heartfelt gratitude to Hope Bible Institute for instilling in me the spiritual foundations that have shaped not only my personal journey but also the heart of this book. Your teaching, guidance, and unwavering commitment to the spiritual aspects of life have deeply influenced me, and I am honored to acknowledge the role you have played in this work.

To my wonderful spouse, Dr. Kendolyn A. Wright, Thank you for standing beside me through every step of this journey. Your unwavering love, patience, and encouragement have been my foundation, and I could not have done this without you.

To my children, twin daughters, Shantea R. Calhoun and Shanea M. Calhoun, Thank you for the incredible gift of parenthood. Through you, I have learned the depths of love, the challenges of raising a family, and the beauty of resilience.

To my pastor, Dr. Ralph M. McCormick, your leadership, wisdom, and faith have been my guiding light. Your words have uplifted me in times of doubt and strengthened my spirit when I needed it most.

To my coach, Casidy Sanders, Thank you for pushing me beyond my limits and reminding me of my own strength. Your guidance has been instrumental in this journey.

To my book coach, Wanda Coleman, Thank you for believing in me when I struggled to believe in myself. Your encouragement, insights, and faith in my vision helped me through this chapter of life.

To all who have supported me, whether through words, prayers, or actions, I am forever grateful. This book is a testament to the love, wisdom, and encouragement I have received, and I hope it will serve as a source of inspiration for others.

CONTENTS

FOREWORD

I would like to take a moment to express my sincere gratitude to Dr. Kendolyn A. Wright for her guidance, encouragement, and assistance during the development of this book. Her support in helping shape several chapters, offering insight, and providing thoughtful feedback played a meaningful role in bringing this project to completion.

Throughout the writing process, Kendolyn offered not only her knowledge and experience but also her patience and dedication to the message behind this work. Her ability to help organize thoughts, strengthen content, and keep the focus on the purpose of helping families and children made a lasting impact on this book.

This project was deeply personal, and having someone who believed in the vision and was willing to walk alongside me during the writing journey made the process much more meaningful. I am grateful for her time, her wisdom, and her willingness to assist where it was needed, while always respecting that the heart of this story comes from lived experience.

It is my hope that this book will help parents, families, and children who find themselves in the middle of difficult situations, and I appreciate those who supported me behind the scenes to help make this message possible.

— Deloris Calhoun-Wright

PREFACE

I decided to write this book because it wasn't until I became a grandmother that I truly understood what co-parenting is, what it means, what it requires, and how deeply it can affect a child. As a young teenage mother, co-parenting was not something I practiced or even thought about. It wasn't a priority between my children's father and me. Growing up without my biological father and being raised instead by a stepfather, I didn't have a model to follow. I simply learned to survive, not realizing that my children were silently learning from everything I didn't know. Then life came in full circle when I became a grandmother.

Now, my role brings me back to the same emotional strain but just from the opposite side of the circle. I can say I have wisdom instead of uncertainty. Where there was once survival mode, I now have a different perspective. Where there was fear, now there's compassion. I recognize the challenges because I have lived them.

Becoming a grandparent opened my eyes in a way I never expected, as I watched my daughters navigate their own co-parenting journeys with the fathers of their children. I saw the strain, the miscommunication, the misunderstandings, the frustrations, and the constant tug of war that can put a child right in the middle. (Co-Parenting Gone Wrong... lol.)

I also saw moments of progress, grace, and growth, the times when respect, flexibility, and teamwork made all the difference.

As I saw the ups and the downs unfold from the outside looking in, I realized something was truly missing. Something was broken. Not just in our family, because I began to notice so many families struggling to raise children between two homes.

I felt a pull in my spirit, a responsibility to speak honestly about co-parenting, not from perfection but from experience, observation, and truth. This book was birthed from that place.

In writing this book, my goal is not to judge or shame anyone. Instead, my goal is to shine a light on what co-parenting really takes, which is communication that is clear, concise, and consistent.
Respect, even when you don't agree.
Flexibility when life shifts.
And a commitment to doing what is best for the child, ALWAYS.

This book is my way of breaking cycles, breaking generational curses, starting conversations, and offering healing where there has been hurt. It is a reminder that the child should never be caught in the crossfire but lifted in love by both parents, together or apart.

I wrote this book to keep co-parenting real. I wrote it for my children, my grandchildren, for every family trying to get it right, and I wrote it for you.

INTRODUCTION

Co-parenting is one of the most important responsibilities a parent can face. Whether it is due to divorce, separation, or other life circumstances, parents raising a child while living apart require patience, effective communication, and respect.

Co-parenting is about building a strong partnership, being collaborative, and working intentionally to raise children together, regardless of relationship status. It requires communication that is clear, concise, and consistent. It is a shared commitment to mutual respect, responsibility, and support for a child's well-being and emotional growth.

Co-parenting is not about maintaining a perfect relationship. Instead, it is about creating a positive and nurturing environment where children feel loved, supported, and able to grow, even when they live in separate homes.

Building a strong co-parenting relationship can be challenging, especially when parents are navigating emotional feelings, conflict, differences, and parenting styles. Yet when both parents focus on the shared goal of the child's well-being, a healthy and supportive relationship becomes possible. This partnership requires open communication, respect for one another, and the willingness to set aside personal disagreements for the sake of the child.

This book is dedicated to exploring how parents can work together harmoniously, ensuring that their children feel secure, loved, and supported, regardless of the dynamics between adults.

"Your child is your lifeline for a lifetime."
— *Deloris Calhoun-Wright, 2026*

CHAPTER 1

FOUNDATIONS OF CO-PARENTING:

BUILDING A STRONG PARTNERSHIP

Co-parenting is rarely the picture parents hold in their hearts when they imagine raising a child. Most expect unity, partnership, and a shared journey that lasts a lifetime. Yet, life sometimes unfolds differently. Relationships change, marriages end, or a connection may never have fully formed. But, at the end of these outcomes, the child remains. The child did not ask for conflict, separation, or divided households. They simply want to feel safe, supported, and loved by both parents.

A healthy co-parenting partnership begins with an understanding that the goal is not to win an argument, prove a point, or revisit past pain. It is about building a strong foundation that protects the child's emotional and psychological well-being. That foundation functions like the supporting beams of a house. If those beams are weak or broken, the structure will not hold. A co-parenting relationship, when built with care and consistency, can withstand many disagreements, storms, and complex seasons of life.

At the heart of this foundation is communication. Co-parenting requires communication that is concise, consistent, clear, and compassionate. Communication must be honest and respectfully centered on the needs of the child, not the wounds of the past. Parents will need to discuss matters involving the child's health, school performance, routines, friendships, and emotional well-being. When communication is handled with maturity and care, the child learns that love can remain, even when relationships change.

Children experience the world through patterns and predictability. They feel more secure when expectations are similar in both households. Although every home has its own personality, it helps when bedtime, daily routines, screen time, homework expectations, and basic rules remain steady. This consistency reduces anxiety and provides confidence and emotional safety. Children do not need identical homes, but they benefit deeply when they can rely on a similar structure, support, and care. I feel that if both parents would allow the child to have the same routines across both households, that would reduce anxiety and promote stability, consistency and an emotionally safe environment.

Co-parenting also requires parents to manage their own emotions responsibly. Separation, disappointment, and frustration are real experiences, and it is natural for parents to feel the emotions that may come with them. Yet a choice must still be made, and parents must ask themselves: Will I respond from my emotions, or from my responsibility as a parent? When adults allow anger or resentment to guide decisions, children become silent carriers of a burden that never belonged to them.

A child should not be used as a messenger or placed in the middle of adult disagreements. The issues between parents are adult issues, and the child deserves protection, not pressure.

A child-centered approach means always asking the following question: What is best for the child, not what is easiest for me? Children need space to express their feelings without fear. They need reassurance that it is acceptable and healthy to love both parents. They should never feel that expressing affection for one parent will hurt the other. Their hearts should remain free and unrestricted.

Another important part of co-parenting is recognizing the shift from a romantic relationship to a parenting partnership. This transition can feel uncomfortable or emotional, especially when heartbreak or unfinished conversations linger in the background. It can help to reflect on a simple truth: even if the relationship did not continue, the love that brought the child into the world still matters. Parenting becomes a shared assignment, even if the relationship has changed form. Respect does not require closeness, but it does require maturity.

Part of my understanding of co-parenting comes from my own story. I often return to memories of my childhood and the absence of my father. My mother never had the opportunity to co-parent with him. A simple misunderstanding led to years of distance, and that separation shaped my identity, my confidence, and how I viewed myself in the world. Growing up without a father left an empty space where guidance and presence should have been. When I became a young parent myself, I had not yet learned from that experience. My children's father was available to assist with co-parenting despite our young age; however, I was fortunate to have a wonderful mother and a strong support system that enabled me to raise my children independently. However, as I was raising my twins, I was overwhelmed and unaware that one day my children would grow up and carry the effects of decisions I made before I fully understood them.

Today, as a grandmother, I see co-parenting differently. Time and wisdom have softened my view and expanded my understanding. I see now how powerful, healing, and life-changing co-parenting can be when it is built on respect, love, and a shared commitment to a child's well-being. I see how offering a child access to both parents, when safe and appropriate, is a gift that strengthens their identity and sense of belonging.

In some co-parenting situations, trust has been damaged. Broken promises, abandonment, betrayal, or past harm may make cooperation difficult. Healing will take time, and it may require outside support through counseling, mediation, or a licensed mental health therapist. Trust is not rebuilt through words alone but through accountability, honesty, and consistent follow-through.

Co-parenting may also become more complex when new relationships or blended families form. These situations call for patience and sensitivity. A new partner in a child's life should be introduced with care, respect, and clarity about roles. A stepparent is not a replacement for a biological parent but can become an added source of love and support. Comparing households or fueling competition can disrupt a child's sense of stability. Children benefit when all adults create an environment where they are encouraged, supported, and free to form healthy bonds.

Healthy co-parenting relationships can often be seen in everyday moments. A child who struggles in school may receive encouragement from both parents, each reinforcing progress rather than blaming the other. A milestone, whether a lost tooth or a graduation, becomes a shared celebration rather than a moment of tension. Even when parents do not attend events together, they can still show unity through supportive words and a child-centered presence. These moments shape a child's inner world. They help a child understand that, although the family structure changed, their heart is still held by people who care.

As you reflect on your own journey, you may consider what parts of your heart still need healing. You may think about how your child would describe the way you treat their other parent, or what legacy you hope your child remembers when they look back on their upbringing. Co-parenting is not just a present-day responsibility; it becomes a part of a family's history and a powerful influence on future generations.

There is no perfect co-parenting plan and no parent who will get it right every time. What matters is a willingness to grow, to listen, and to work toward peace. Co-parenting is a continuous practice of grace, patience, humility, and hope.

The goal is for the child to grow up feeling not like someone caught in the middle, but like someone lifted by love on all sides.

When parents commit to clear and respectful communication, emotional maturity, and a child-centered focus, the structure of co-parenting becomes strong enough to hold the family through change. The foundation laid today affects how a child will form relationships, how they will trust, how they will heal, and how they will love.

If the beams are strong, the home will stand. And inside that home, the child can flourish, knowing they were worth every effort, every conversation, every moment of patience, and every choice to love beyond personal feelings. In this way, co-parenting is not simply a shared responsibility. It is an act of protection, of legacy, and of unconditional care for the child in the middle.

CHAPTER 2

PUTTING THE CHILD FIRST:

PRIORITIZING THEIR WELL-BEING WHILE FOCUSING

ON THE CHILD'S BEST INTEREST

There are moments in life when you look back and finally see the pattern. You see the threads that were woven long before you took your first breath, shaping you, stretching you, and preparing you to speak on something that most people avoid. My journey with co-parenting did not begin when I became a mother; it began when I was a child, standing in the middle of adults who could not figure out how to work together for my sake. The lessons that shaped my life came from watching, waiting, longing, and eventually learning what it means to prioritize a child's heart above every misunderstanding.

This chapter is my story. It is the truth of where I come from, what I survived, and why this book exists. Every part of my life, from Alabama to Connecticut, from childhood to motherhood, from brokenness to strength, has taught me that putting the child first is possible. Healing is possible. Breaking generational patterns is possible. But we must first be willing to see the child in the middle and make decisions that honor them and not our hurt.

Early Roots: Alabama and the First Signs of Co-Parenting Struggles

My story begins in the warm red clay of Alabama. I was just a little girl trying to make sense of the world around me. Some of my earliest memories are not of playgrounds or schoolrooms, but of my older brother taking my hand and leading me to see my father's sisters. Those visits were not planned by adults. They were not the result of communication or cooperation. They were made possible by a child trying to help another child stay connected to her roots.

For a significant part of my early years, I lived with my grandmother, Big Mama. My mother eventually moved to Connecticut after a misunderstanding with my father, and that decision shifted the entire structure of my childhood. I stayed behind in Alabama, living in the same state as my father, yet never seeing him. The lines of communication between my parents were thin, strained, or nonexistent. Because of that, the connection between my father and me never existed.

When communication fails, children suffer in silence. Co-parenting requires communication, even if the parents no longer share a relationship. When I was 6 years old, I didn't understand why I wasn't being picked up or why I barely saw the other side of my family. I didn't have the vocabulary for grief or longing, but I felt it. I experienced the missing pieces before I knew what they were.

My brother, at the age of 18, did what adults should have done, taught me my first lesson about co-parenting. Children should never have to fill in the gaps parents leave behind. Yet many children do, and many children carry those emotional responsibilities into adulthood without ever realizing the weight they have been holding.

Eventually, my sisters and I moved to Connecticut to be with our mother. It was a big transition for us, leaving the familiarity of Alabama and stepping into a new place, a new environment, and eventually, a blended family. My mother remarried, and this relationship introduced another version of co-parenting into my life.

My stepfather was physically present but emotionally absent. He wasn't mean, and he wasn't harmful, but he wasn't engaged. He did not attend our school events, guide us through challenges, or invest in our growth. My mother carried the entire weight of parenting on her shoulders. She cooked, cleaned, nurtured, and provided. She was our stability. She was our support. She was our everything.

What I learned from this season was that co-parenting is not defined by titles. Someone can hold the title of stepparent and still not be a co-parent. Presence without participation is just another form of absence. Children need connection, not just a body in the room.

That experience showed me that blended families require intentionality. Love is not automatic; relationships must be built on trust, shared values, and the willingness to show up consistently. Without that, children grow up feeling unseen in their own homes.

Meeting My Father Too Late

One of the hardest truths of my life is that I did not truly meet my father until I was in my late thirties. For decades, I carried questions, hopes, and empty spaces where memories should have been. When I finally met him, the reunion was meaningful, emotional, and necessary. But it was also bittersweet. Not long after reconnecting, he passed away.

I grieved the loss, but I also grieved the years. The missed moments. The what ifs. The childhood, teenage years, and young adulthood I spent without the man who helped bring me into this world.

Meeting my father so late in life showed me the depth of what co-parenting failures can take from a child. When adults allow conflict or pride to keep them from working together, the child pays the price in lost relationships, lost identity, and lost time that can never be replaced.

Becoming a Mother and Facing Familiar Patterns

I became a mother at a young age, full of dreams of giving my children everything I didn't have. I imagined a cooperative parenting relationship, one where both parents showed up, supported each other, and stood unified for the sake of the child. But life doesn't always unfold the way we envision.

Two years after the twins were born, my relationship with my children's father ended, and his involvement diminished. He entered a new relationship, and soon it became clear that his new partner did not want him interacting with me, even when it involved our children. That tension created distance between him and the girls, a distance that should never exist between a father and his children.

I found myself stepping into the same pattern I witnessed as a child: making excuses, covering his absence, protecting his image so my children wouldn't feel rejected. For instance, when I would buy gifts for the girls, and while giving them, I would say, "This is from your dad," even when it wasn't. I would reassure them that he was coming when deep down I knew he wasn't. I carried the emotional burden to spare their hearts, not realizing that I was also teaching them a harmful pattern. Children learn from what we model, not just what we say.

Through this experience, I learned that covering for another parent is not co-parenting. True co-parenting is accountability. For both parents, it is showing up. It is being honest. It is prioritizing the child even when the adult relationship is difficult or nonexistent.

When I eventually got married, I experienced a season of support and partnership that helped heal some of the wounds from my past. My husband wasn't my children's biological father, but he genuinely stepped into the role of father from the moment he entered our lives. He was present, attentive, and invested in my daughters' well-being. He supported them in ways that many biological fathers never do. He helped raise them, guide them, and love them without hesitation or condition.

Even though our marriage ended, his contribution to their lives was meaningful and lasting. His presence gave them a glimpse of what healthy, stable fatherhood could look like, and for that, I will always be grateful.

Later, in my second marriage, I encountered another type of challenge. My second husband was controlling, creating an environment where co-parenting was more about authority than partnership. My children felt that tension deeply. Even when they could not name it, they sensed imbalance and dominance. I also experienced significant issues because the continued highly controlling, authoritative behaviors negatively affected the emotional environment. As a stepparent, his approach created tension and stress for the children and interfered with healthy communication. It had a huge impact on their emotional well-being and emotional instability. From him, I learned what co-parenting should not be: rigid, fear-based, or control-driven.

These experiences taught me that healthy co-parenting is impossible without emotional intelligence, mutual respect, and humility. It is not about who is in charge, but about who is willing to collaborate.

Watching My Children Repeat the Cycle

My daughters grew to be strong, educated, accomplished women. They received honors in school, excelled in sports, and have earned both bachelor's and master's degrees. They are now amazing mothers, professionals, and human beings. But even the strongest among us can carry unspoken wounds from childhood.

I have watched my daughters struggle with co-parenting in similar ways to what I experienced. I've seen them cover for absentee fathers, hold their families together alone, and face the stress that comes with trying to co-parent with someone who may be inconsistent, emotionally unavailable, or influenced by outside relationships. I realize now how much they learned from watching me, even when I didn't know they were watching.

This is why generational cycles matter. Children absorb the patterns they see. If we do not heal what hurts us, we unintentionally pass it along. That realization is one of the driving forces behind this book.

Healing, Accountability, and Putting the Child First

Healthy co-parenting is built on a foundation of mutual respect, regardless of relationship status. Parents do not have to be friends, but they do have to be responsible. They must communicate clearly, manage their emotions, and avoid using the child as a weapon or a bargaining tool.

Healing plays a powerful role. Many co-parenting challenges come from unresolved hurt, heartbreak, ego, or fear. When adults hold onto bitterness, the child becomes the casualty. But when adults choose healing, forgiveness, and emotional maturity, the child becomes the beneficiary.

Putting the child first means making decisions based on what is truly best for them, not what satisfies an emotional response from the parent. It means ensuring the child is loved, supported, nurtured, and guided. It means creating a stable environment, fostering secure connections, and encouraging healthy relationships with both sides of the family whenever possible.

Guiding Principles for Healthy Co-Parenting

Healthy co-parenting is not about perfection. It is about commitment, consistency, and compassion. Even in complicated situations, parents can adopt guiding principles that protect the child's emotional well-being.

Healthy communication is essential. Speaking calmly, clearly, and respectfully sets the tone for cooperation. It prevents misunderstandings and reduces conflict. Children thrive when they see adults communicating with maturity.

Emotional intelligence matters. Parents must recognize their emotions, handle conflict with self-control, and avoid projecting frustration onto the child. When parents regulate themselves, children feel safe.

Mutual respect forms the foundation for stability. Parents can disagree without being disrespectful. Respect builds trust, trust builds consistency, and consistency builds emotional safety for the child.

Shared values help guide decisions. Even if the parents live separately, agreeing on routines, discipline, education, and expectations helps the child experience unity.

Conflict resolution is key. Children should never witness intense arguments or feel responsible for adult problems. Healthy conflict resolution teaches them how to solve problems constructively.

Partnership dynamics create opportunities. Parents who willingly collaborate can share responsibilities, alternate tasks, attend school events together, and provide the child with a sense of security that transcends relationship status.

These principles may not erase all challenges, but they create a path forward where the child is protected and valued.

Breaking the Cycle for Future Generations

When I look at my life, I see three generations affected by broken co-parenting: my mother and father, me and my children's father, and my daughters and their children's fathers. These patterns have stretched across decades, shaping identities and relationships. But patterns can be broken. Cycles can end. Healing can begin with one person deciding to make a different choice.

That person is me. And it can be you.

This chapter is more than a reflection. It is a declaration. It is an invitation to choose better for our children. It is a reminder that what we model is what they become. When we choose maturity, peace, and collaboration, our children learn how to build those same qualities in their own relationships.

Putting the child first is not a slogan. It is a commitment. It is a lifestyle. It is a promise that no matter what the adult relationship looks like, the child will not suffer because of it.

A Final Word of Hope

I wrote this book because I believe change is possible. I have lived in every corner of co-parenting. I have been the child in the middle, the mother trying her best, and the grandmother watching the cycle repeat. I know the pain, the disappointment, the exhaustion, and the fear. But I also know the power of awareness, the strength of healing, and the beauty of transformation.

Putting the child first can change everything. It can restore connections, rebuild trust, and rewrite generational stories.

It can protect the innocence and emotional health of children who deserve to grow up without carrying adult burdens.

I want families to know that it can be done. It takes willingness, patience, and humility, but it is possible. This chapter is my truth, and my truth is an offering to every parent trying to navigate co-parenting with grace.

Let this be the moment where we stand together and choose to prioritize our children's well-being above everything else. They deserve that. And we are capable of giving it.

CHAPTER 3

EFFECTIVE COMMUNICATION:
KEYS TO STAYING ON THE SAME PAGE

Healthy co-parenting begins with communication rooted in respect, clarity, and compassion. When two parents commit to raising a child together, even from separate households or through seasons of conflict, their ability to communicate well becomes one of the strongest foundations supporting the child's emotional well-being. Communication is more than exchanging information. It is listening with intention, speaking with care, and approaching each conversation with the understanding that you are building a long-term parenting partnership for the sake of your child.

At the heart of co-parenting communication is a willingness to be open and honest. Children feel the emotional atmosphere created by their parents, even when the parents assume they don't notice. They observe tone, body language, and the level of peace or tension between their parents. When parents communicate respectfully, they create a sense of stability that follows the child from home to home, reminding them that they are loved, supported, and secure despite whatever has changed in the adult relationship.

Respect serves as the cornerstone of effective co-parenting. This involves avoiding passive-aggressive statements, sarcasm, blame, and emotionally charged comments that escalate tension. It also means maintaining a calm, neutral tone even when the topic feels difficult. Respect in communication shows the child that their parents can work through challenges without tearing each other down. It models emotional intelligence and teaches them how to manage conflict in their own lives with dignity and grace. Even when disagreements occur, responding with respect communicates a powerful message: our child comes first.

Open, honest information sharing is essential for keeping both parents aligned. Withholding information, even unintentionally, can create frustration and mistrust. Co-parenting requires consistent updates about the child's health, school performance, routines, emotional changes, and any shifts in living arrangements. Each parent has a right and responsibility to know where their child lives, who they spend time with, and what is happening in their daily life. When one parent is kept in the dark, it disrupts the partnership and places unnecessary pressure on the child. Sharing information promptly, even when it seems minor, promotes unity and prevents misunderstandings that could otherwise harm the relationship.

One of the most damaging habits in strained co-parenting relationships is slipping into a winning mindset. Parenting is not a competition, and there are no rewards for proving a point or being "right" at the expense of peace. The true win is when the child feels emotionally safe and supported. Additionally, choosing cooperation over conflict allows both parents to focus on what truly matters. Compromise is often necessary and is a sign of emotional maturity, not weakness. Therefore, placing the child's long-term well-being above personal pride strengthens the co-parenting relationship and reduces unnecessary tension.

Consistency between households plays a major role in providing emotional security for children. When rules, boundaries, and expectations are wildly different between homes, children can become confused or anxious. While each household will naturally reflect the parents' individual style, key principles such as bedtime routines, discipline approaches, screen time guidelines, and homework expectations should remain relatively aligned. Consistency does not mean the homes must be identical. Instead, it means that both parents respect each other's roles and are committed to offering the child a stable rhythm they can depend on. Even when disagreements arise, striving toward alignment reinforces cooperation.

Flexibility is also important in co-parenting. Life happens, and unexpected situations may require changes to visitation schedules or daily routines. Being open to adjustments when emergencies or unavoidable conflicts arise shows goodwill and reduces strain. Flexibility should be balanced with consistency, so the child still experiences routine, but extending grace to one another during challenging moments helps the partnership remain functional and peaceful. Communicating honestly and respectfully about changes prevents misunderstanding and strengthens trust.

In moments of tension or strong emotion, structured communication becomes a useful tool. This does not mean formal scripts or rigid rules, but rather an intentional approach that keeps conversations focused and respectful. Remaining calm, speaking from a personal perspective rather than accusation, staying on topic, and pausing when emotions escalate help prevent conflict from spiraling. Structured communication protects both parents from unnecessary harm and preserves the co-parenting relationship even during difficult seasons.

Regular check-ins can also support healthy communication. These check-ins might occur weekly, bi-weekly, or monthly, depending on what works best for the family. Check-ins on a regular basis, like phone calls daily, video calls, when possible, a discussion of schedules, and sometimes just showing up is very impactful. Also, checks in on homework, doctor's appointments, and changes in behaviors provide a predictable space to share updates about the child's school progress, friendships, emotional health, and any concerns. Consistent conversations prevent resentment from building and keep both parents operating as partners rather than isolated individuals trying to make decisions alone. Regular communication does not require deep friendship between parents; it simply requires mutual respect and commitment to the child's best interests.

A vital part of communication in co-parenting is creating space for children to express their emotions. Children need permission to speak openly about their experiences without feeling they must protect one parent from the other. When parents communicate well, children feel freer to share their worries, excitement, or disappointments. Encouraging emotional openness helps children develop resilience and trust. Listening without judgment reinforces their sense of belonging in both homes.

Emotional intelligence is a powerful skill in co-parenting. It involves managing your own emotions, understanding the emotions of others, and responding thoughtfully rather than reactively. This can be challenging, especially when the parenting relationship carries history, hurt, or unresolved conflict. But emotional intelligence helps parents slow down, consider the impact of their words, and choose responses that support peace rather than provoke tension. It requires self-awareness and a willingness to pause before reacting. When parents practice emotional intelligence, they create an environment where the child feels safe and where conversations become opportunities for growth rather than confrontation.

For parents who are trying to rebuild trust after conflict or separation, communication becomes both a challenge and an opportunity. Trust is not rebuilt through demands but through consistent behavior. When parents demonstrate reliability, follow through on commitments, share information openly, and speak respectfully, trust gradually begins to grow. Even when forgiveness is still a work in progress, consistency creates emotional safety. Children benefit when their parents choose patience and persistence in healing the co-parenting relationship.

Some co-parenting relationships are extremely difficult. When there is ongoing tension, differences in values, or unresolved emotional wounds, communication may require clear boundaries. In these cases, keeping messages brief, focused, and factual can prevent conflict from escalating. Also, using written communication, when necessary, provides clarity and avoids misunderstandings. Focusing strictly on the child's needs and stepping away when the conversation becomes emotionally charged can help maintain stability. In certain circumstances, involving a mediator or counselor may assist both parents in developing healthier communication practices. Progress may be gradual, but even small improvements can significantly benefit the child.

Furthermore, blended families add another layer to the co-parenting journey. New partners, stepsiblings, and expanded family roles can shift routines and responsibilities. Clear communication becomes even more important during these transitions. Children may need reassurance that new relationships do not replace their bond with either parent. Respecting each other's roles and acknowledging new dynamics without competition creates harmony and emotional safety. When blended families approach communication with openness, humility, and sensitivity, children gain a broader network of support.

Child-focused decision-making should remain the guiding principle in every co-parenting conversation. This means consistently asking how each decision will affect the child's emotional and physical well-being. When parents prioritize the child's needs above personal conflict, they create an environment where the child can grow confidently and peacefully. Child-focused decision-making reminds parents to pause, breathe, and choose what serves the child rather than what satisfies a momentary feeling.

Healthy co-parenting dynamics are built on respect, cooperation, consistency, and openness. When parents communicate with these values in mind, they support the child's emotional health and strengthen the parenting partnership. Problematic dynamics such as withholding information, speaking negatively about the other parent, using the child as a messenger, or competing for affection can create unnecessary stress. Awareness and willingness to change these patterns can restore balance and improve communication.

Strengthening the co-parenting relationship is an ongoing process. It grows through small, intentional acts of kindness such as expressing appreciation for the other parent's efforts, acknowledging their contributions, or offering support during challenging times. These gestures do not erase the past but build a healthier future. Co-parenting is not about perfection. It is about showing up, communicating with care, and choosing peace whenever possible.

In the end, effective communication is a form of love expressed on behalf of the child. It is the daily decision to build bridges rather than walls. It is choosing stability over conflict and cooperation over pride. No matter how complicated the journey has been, it is always possible to create a healthier, more supportive partnership. Your child will remember the stability you created and the respect you demonstrated. They will remember the love you prioritized above everything else.

Co-parenting communication is a lifelong journey of healing, growth, and shared purpose. Every step you take strengthens the emotional foundation your child is standing on. You are not just communicating; you are shaping the kind of world your child will grow up in, one where they feel safe, loved, and deeply supported by both of their parents.

Reflection Questions

1. Consider moments in your communication with your co-parent that felt respectful, calm, and productive. What made those conversations work well, and how can you carry those strengths into future discussions?

2. Think about a recent disagreement or misunderstanding. How might the outcome have changed if the conversation had centered more on the child's needs rather than the emotions of the moment?

3. Reflect on how your child responds when communication between you and your co-parent is peaceful versus when it is tense. What does this reveal about the importance of maintaining stability and emotional safety?

4. Reflect on how you respond under stress. Do you tend to withdraw, shut down, or become defensive? How can emotional intelligence help you respond more thoughtfully?

5. Think about the bigger picture of your co-parenting journey. What values do you want your child to remember about how their parents worked together?

CHAPTER 4

ESTABLISHING BOUNDARIES,

ROLES, & RESPECT

Healthy co-parenting does not happen by accident. It grows from intention, emotional maturity, and a clear understanding of what both parents need to create stability for the child. Establishing boundaries and practicing respect are two of the most essential elements in building a strong and functional co-parenting partnership. Without them, communication becomes strained, misunderstandings increase, and the child often ends up feeling caught in the middle of unresolved adult conflict. With boundaries and respect, however, a co-parenting relationship can evolve into a peaceful, supportive, and consistent environment where the child feels secure and emotionally safe.

Co-parents must learn to respect each other's time, personal space, and differing viewpoints. Each household has its own rhythms and its own ways of managing daily life. No two parents, regardless of their past relationship, will agree on everything. But respect bridges the gap between differences. When both parents feel heard and valued, cooperation increases naturally. Clear boundaries help each parent understand what is expected, what is acceptable, and what crosses the line. This clarity reduces unnecessary conflict and strengthens the emotional foundation that both parents are trying to build for their child.

Boundaries do not have to be complicated. In fact, some of the most effective boundaries are simple, direct, and rooted in common sense. When you set boundaries, they should make sense for the child's well-being and for the smooth functioning of both households. Boundaries that are clear allow both parents to navigate their roles without confusion or resentment. Healthy co-parenting boundaries focus on decision-making, communication, time management, and respect for each other's parenting styles and responsibilities. These boundaries protect the emotional health of the child and strengthen trust between parents.

The heart of co-parenting is always the child. When parents place the child's needs above personal grievances, pride, or emotional triggers, the co-parenting dynamic becomes more stable and supportive. Prioritizing the child means remembering that the child is the one experiencing the back-and-forth between households. The child is the one absorbing the emotional temperature of the home and the tension between the adults. The child is the one learning how to communicate, set boundaries, and form relationships based on the example the parents provide. When boundaries are honored, the child becomes the beneficiary of a peaceful and predictable environment. This is why boundaries must always be centered on what is best for the child, not on scoring points or proving a personal argument.

Co-parenting involves recognizing that flexibility is necessary. Rigid rules and inflexible routines create unnecessary tension and limit the child's ability to adapt. Flexibility does not mean giving up boundaries or allowing disrespect. Instead, flexibility means allowing room for life to happen. Everything will not always go as planned. Schedules may shift. Emergencies arise. Special events come up. When parents approach these moments with grace and understanding, they model the kind of emotional intelligence they hope to cultivate in their child. Compromise becomes easier when both parents know that the goal is not personal convenience but the child's well-being. In real life, it would be wonderful if parents could exercise emotional intelligence when circumstances arise beyond their control by concentrating on the solution and not the problem. Parents need to stay respectful, calm and neutral to help reduce the child's anxiety. These displays of emotional intelligence teach the child resilience, not avoidance. For example, what my daughter has been teaching my grandson is that feelings don't have to equal chaos. Emotions can be managed without exploding.

There will be moments when misunderstandings occur, and boundaries are tested or even violated. In these moments, how parents respond will determine whether the conflict grows or gets resolved. Respecting each other's boundaries means choosing to communicate with clarity rather than anger and choosing to seek understanding rather than assuming the worst. When both parents know that their voice matters and that their concerns will be heard, they are more likely to respond with cooperation instead of defensiveness. This mutual respect becomes the foundation for lasting trust.

One of the hardest lessons in co-parenting is accepting that not everyone comes into the co-parenting relationship with the same emotional tools or communication skills. Some parents may struggle with self-control, consistency, or emotional regulation. Others may come into co-parenting with past hurt, unhealed trauma, or lingering resentment. When these challenges are combined with unclear boundaries, exchanges can quickly escalate into conflict. Many parents have had moments where a small misunderstanding spiraled into an argument, not because of the child, but because boundaries were never clearly defined.

A personal experience of mine occurred standing at a figurative and literal crossroad, sick to my stomach, on what should have been an ordinary Friday. What should have been a simple conversation, guided by a little flexibility and understanding, ended with police involvement because boundaries were unclear. This kind of moment stays with a parent. It becomes a turning point; a powerful reminder of how urgently boundaries are needed and how vulnerable a child becomes when parents lack structure.

It was my daughter's scheduled weekend to have her son. The father had already kept him for an additional week prior to my daughter willingly giving up so their son could join his father on a family vacation. When they returned, instead of bringing him back home to his mother as expected, the father took him to his own residence.

My daughter contacted him to let him know she was coming to pick up her son. He had never provided his home address, so she had to obtain it after hearing it verified aloud during a recent doctor's visit. She arrived and remained parked on the street, not in the driveway, simply to pick up her child.

However, the father refused to let their son leave the house, stating that she had no right to come to his home. His wife added that "boundaries needed to be set." Left with no other option, my daughter called the police. Once officers confirmed that there was a joint custody agreement in place, they spoke with the father inside the home while my daughter waited in her car. Only then did he allow Kaleb to come outside.

The situation raised an important question: why was law enforcement necessary for a mother to retrieve her child during her court-recognized parenting time?

The lesson from that experience is clear. When boundaries are missing, even simple interactions can escalate into chaos. When boundaries are in place, uncertainty transforms into stability, and fear gives way to peace. The child should never be caught in the middle of emotional storms that could have been avoided with honest communication and mutual respect.

Establishing and maintaining boundaries is not just about preventing conflict. It is about building a foundation of trust, consistency, and emotional safety that benefits the child's long-term development. When parents respect boundaries, they create a predictable rhythm that helps the child feel grounded. Children thrive in environments where rules make sense, routines are consistent, and adults handle conflict with maturity. They watch how their parents speak to each other, how they manage disagreements, and how they protect each other's dignity. This becomes the blueprint for how they will build relationships in their own lives.

The phrase the child in the middle speaks directly to the heart of co-parenting. Children often absorb tension long before they understand it. They notice raised voices, silent treatments, dismissive tones, and emotional distance. They feel the weight of arguments even if they do not hear every word. When parents fight or fail to communicate respectfully, the child's emotional stability is shaken. Co-parenting is not about the convenience of adults. It is about shielding the child from unnecessary stress and ensuring they feel loved unconditionally in both homes.

The reality is that not all co-parenting relationships begin from a place of peace. Some begin with heartbreak. Some begin in courtrooms. Some begin with mistrust or disappointment. And some begin with patterns that were never healthy to begin with. But no matter how the journey starts, healthy boundaries can turn even difficult co-parenting relationships into safe and functional partnerships. Boundaries create clarity. Clarity creates trust. Trust creates stability. And stability creates emotional safety for the child.

Respect is not earned through dominance or control. When parents see each other fulfilling responsibilities with intention, trust naturally increases. The co-parenting relationship becomes more predictable, more balanced, and more peaceful.

How Respect is Earned

- Showing up on time for exchanges
- Honoring agreed-upon schedules
- Respecting each other's personal lives
- Keeping communication focused on the child
- Following through on promises

Even in blended families, boundaries remain essential. When new relationships or additional children enter the picture, clarity becomes even more important. Boundaries help new partners understand their roles and prevent misunderstandings that could create tension between households. Healthy blended-family boundaries include respecting the primary parent's authority, supporting the child's emotional connection to both biological parents, and avoiding behaviors that make the child feel torn or conflicted. Blended families thrive when adults communicate openly, compassionately, and honestly about roles, expectations, and transitions.

Boundaries also protect the co-parenting relationship from unnecessary emotional triggers. For many parents, the past relationship carries wounds that resurface unexpectedly. Boundaries provide a way to navigate communication without stepping into old patterns. They create emotional separation while allowing collaboration for the child's benefit. A boundary can be as simple as communicating only through text or email when emotions run high or agreeing to discuss sensitive topics only during designated times when both parents can speak calmly and clearly. Boundaries safeguard emotional well-being by reducing opportunities for conflict to arise.

Conflict is not always avoidable, even with boundaries. However, conflict can be managed in ways that do not harm the child or the co-parenting partnership. When a conflict arises, focusing on the facts rather than emotions helps both parents move toward resolution. Conflict becomes manageable when parents choose to express themselves with honesty rather than hostility, and when they listen with the intention to understand rather than to argue. The goal is not to win. The goal is to build a path forward that supports the child's emotional and physical health.

Child-focused decision-making remains the guiding principle of all boundaries. When parents ask themselves whether a decision supports the child's stability, emotional health, developmental needs, and sense of belonging, they are more likely to make choices that prioritize love over conflict. Being child-focused does not mean ignoring your own feelings. It means placing the child's well-being at the center of your decisions and communicating in ways that preserve their sense of safety.

Parents sometimes forget how deeply their behavior shapes their child's understanding of relationships. Children who witness respectful communication learn that disagreements can be resolved without harm. Children who observe consistency between households learn resilience and adaptability. Children who see their parents honor boundaries learn how to set boundaries themselves. The emotional skills parents model become the emotional skills the child carries into adulthood.

Two homes can succeed in raising one heart when the adults commit to boundaries that protect the child and respect each other. These homes do not have to be identical to be unified. They do not have to operate exactly the same way to create stability. They simply need to communicate, honor agreements, and approach co-parenting as a partnership rather than a competition.

Establishing boundaries and respect is not a one-time conversation. It is a continuous practice. It requires patience, forgiveness, flexibility, and emotional awareness. It grows stronger over time as both parents learn more about themselves, their communication patterns, and their child's evolving needs. With each step toward healthier communication, both parents contribute to a more secure and peaceful future for their child.

Co-parenting is a journey of healing, growth, and shared responsibility. Even when the road is difficult, parents can choose to rise above their differences for the sake of the child they both love. Boundaries and respect are not restrictions. They are building blocks for harmony, cooperation, and trust. They create the stable environment every child deserves and demonstrate a powerful truth: even when the relationship changes, the commitment to raising a child with love and respect can remain strong.

CHAPTER 5

CONSISTENCY IS KEY: CREATING A STABLE ENVIRONMENT FOR THE CHILD

When building a strong and lasting foundation in any relationship, particularly in co-parenting, there are four essential pillars that act as the beams of a sturdy house: clear, concise, consistent communication. Without these structural supports, the entire framework of the co-parenting relationship is at risk of leaning under pressure or collapsing in moments of strain. Co-parenting is not simply the exchange of children between homes or the coordination of schedules. It is the sacred work of raising emotionally secure, spiritually grounded, and well-adjusted individuals. These 4 C's form the backbone of the partnership, keeping both parents aligned, steady, and focused on what matters most.

Think of communication in co-parenting like the steel reinforcements hidden deep within concrete. You may not always see it, but it is holding the entire structure together from within. Clear communication means speaking truthfully and plainly. It requires honesty without harshness, directness without disrespect, and transparency without hidden agendas. There is no place for passive-aggressive comments, coded messages, or leaving room for misinterpretation. Instead, you have to respond, listen and focus on the facts and not the sarcasm. It is best not to take things personally. Clarity protects both parents from confusion and protects the child from instability. Concise communication then honors time, energy, and emotional capacity. It means saying what needs to be said without unnecessary detours or emotional explosions. It keeps the conversation focused on the child rather than allowing old wounds to resurface. When parents speak concisely, they set boundaries for themselves and create space for healthy patterns of dialogue. Consistent communication is the thread that weaves trust into the relationship. It signals reliability, dependability, and a shared commitment to the child's well-being. Children feel more secure when they see their parents communicating consistently and calmly, even if the parents live separate lives. Consistency models emotional maturity, showing the child that stability is still possible after a family transition.

Open, honest, and routine discussions are essential for the child's physical, emotional, and educational needs. This includes updates on school activities, health concerns, friendships, emotional shifts, and even subtle behavioral patterns. When both parents take the time to discuss the small things, it prevents bigger misunderstandings. Creating a shared plan for the child's well-being ensures that they feel supported, heard, and cherished in both homes. It allows the child to experience unity rather than division.

Navigating Disagreements with Grace

Disagreements will happen; this is an inevitable part of parenting. What truly matters is how these disagreements are handled. When conflict arises, it is important to engage with respect, patience, and emotional intelligence. I can remember when there was a time when my grandson, Kaleb, was enrolled in one extracurricular activity by one parent and at the same time, the other parent had him signed up for a different activity. The conflict wasn't discovered until later, when it became clear that the dates and times overlapped. When my daughter realized that Kaleb's soccer schedule conflicted with the other activity, she approached the situation with his father calmly. Instead of placing blame or criticizing the father for the lack of communication, she simply pointed out the scheduling overlap and how it would impact Kaleb. She emphasized that Kaleb's well-being and ability to participate fully were the priority. Rather than escalating the situation, she suggested a solution by reaching out to the coaches to see if the schedules could be adjusted, as well as switching the dates to accommodate Kaleb's participation. As a result, the conflict was resolved. Kaleb remained in both activities, and both parents maintained mutual respect. They agreed to communicate more clearly in the future regarding schedules to prevent similar conflicts from happening again.

Additionally, never allow frustration to spill over in front of the child. The child should never become the battleground for unresolved adult issues. Disputes should be addressed with calm language and a clear focus on finding solutions. Avoid placing blame or dredging up past mistakes. Instead, keep conversations anchored in the present moment.

Take deep breaths before responding, especially when emotions run high. Practicing emotional regulation is a gift you give to yourself and your child. When each household maintains clearly defined and mutually respected rules, routines, and expectations, the child feels grounded. Emotional consistency between homes creates a sense of safety. Children thrive when they know what to expect and when they see both parents working together, even from different addresses. It is helpful to align on core routines such as bedtime, discipline, meal habits, homework expectations, and screen time. Perfection is not required, nor are identical parenting styles. But harmony is attainable when parents agree on foundational expectations. This alignment shows the child that the adults guiding their life are working in unity rather than in competition.

Building Shared Values and Principles

Think of co-parenting like discipleship in faith. It requires modeling, teaching, consistency, and encouragement. When both parents collaborate in passing on shared values and principles, the child gains a strong moral and emotional compass. Even if daily life looks different in each home, the underlying lessons remain the same. Children learn how to handle challenges by watching how their parents handle them. They learn how to communicate by observing their parents communicating. They learn how to respect others by noticing the level of respect shown between their parents. When parents take responsibility for the example they set, they shape the emotional future of their child. According to the Bible, "Train up a child in the way he should go, and when he is old, he will not depart from it."

Proverbs 22:6 (KJV)

Your child will remember the conversations, the tone of voice, the body language, and the emotional atmosphere far more than they will remember specific disagreements or rules. If a child grows up seeing grace, patience, forgiveness, and maturity modeled between their parents, that becomes the blueprint for their relationships as adults.

Guarding Against Emotional Reactivity

It is natural to feel frustration, especially if the past relationship carried pain, betrayal, or disappointment. But emotional reactions, when left unchecked, can escalate tensions quickly. It is crucial not to allow past hurts to guide present decisions. Reacting to unresolved wounds pulls the child into emotional storms they were never meant to endure. The Bible suggests, "A gentle answer turns away wrath, but a harsh word stirs up anger." Proverbs 15:1 (NIV)

Children are not responsible for soothing adult emotions. They are not messengers, referees, or emotional support systems. They should never be placed in a position where they feel torn between their parents. When you choose emotional responsibility, you lift the weight from their small shoulders. Before responding in moments of tension, pause and ask yourself whether your response reflects who you want to be. Imagine your child watching this moment years from now. Would they see a parent acting with maturity and love, or would they see someone reacting from hurt? This kind of reflection is powerful.

It encourages parents to choose peace over pride and wisdom over impulsiveness.

Modeling Respect, Even in Difficulty

Speaking respectfully about the other parent, even when you disagree, protects your child's heart. Children internalize negative remarks, often believing that criticism of one parent is criticism of them. They may feel forced to take sides or carry guilt for loving both parents. Modeling dignity, forgiveness, and compassion does not mean ignoring hurt or pretending everything is perfect. It means choosing the higher road for the sake of your child's emotional well-being. Respect builds bridges. It creates an atmosphere of peace. It teaches your child that love can remain even when circumstances change. Difficult moments can test our character, but they also give us an opportunity to show respect. Ephesians 4:2 states, "Be completely humble and gentle; be patient, bearing with one another in love" (NIV). Therefore, the scripture teaches us to be completely humble and gentle, patient and bearing with one another in love, it guides us towards responding with compassion instead of conflict. In the event that only one parent is willing to do the work, the only advice I suggest is to focus on only what can be controlled, which is communication, consistency, keeping the child centered, trying to avoid arguments, and protecting your child's stability in maintaining routines & boundaries.

Even when parents disagree, they can still honor each other in the presence of the child. This maturity becomes a blessing that echoes through the child's life, shaping their emotional resilience and relational health.

Rebuilding Trust and Healing Through Partnership

Some co-parenting relationships begin with deep wounds. Trust may feel fragile or even broken. Healing takes time, patience, and consistent effort. While the co-parenting relationship may never return to what it once was, it can become healthier, more stable, and more supportive with intentional communication. Healing happens when both parents commit to being reliable. Showing up on time, honoring agreements, keeping promises, and using respectful communication slowly rebuilds stability. Over time, small acts of responsibility create a safer emotional environment. Trust is not rebuilt through grand gestures but through consistent, everyday choices. When both parents commit to growth, the co-parenting partnership becomes an opportunity for God to restore what felt lost.

Blended Families and Expanding the Circle of Care

Blended families bring beautiful possibilities and unique challenges. New partners, stepsiblings, and expanded households require even more intentional communication. It is important to remember that the child benefits when all adults involved choose collaboration over competition. Approach blended family dynamics with patience and grace. Allow the child time to adjust, and encourage respect for all caregivers involved. Healthy blended families grow from humility, open dialogue, and shared boundaries. Parents can work together to ensure that new partners contribute positively to the child's life while respecting the existing parental roles. Blended families flourish when adults choose peace over ego and cooperation over comparison.

Conclusion: A Legacy of Unity

In the end, the 4 C's of Clear, Concise, Consistent Communication are more than practical strategies. They are a spiritual and emotional commitment. A commitment to doing what is best for your child. A commitment to growth, healing, and emotional maturity. A commitment to unity, even when agreement feels difficult. Let your child see two people who may not have stayed together, but who stayed united for them. Unity does not require a shared household; it requires a shared purpose. Through clear communication, consistent actions and committed co-parenting, a child can witness unity in a powerful way, because overall, this is the legacy that you want to leave with your child. As Psalm 133:1 says, "How good and pleasant it is when people live together in unity" (NIV). Choosing unity for a child's well-being reflects love in action. This is the legacy you leave. A legacy of strength. A legacy of emotional safety. A legacy of love that continues to protect and guide your child for the rest of their life.

CHAPTER 6

WHEN FAMILIES SHIFT: HEALING CONFLICT, TRANSITIONAL GROWING AND BLENDED BEGINNINGS

Transitions are a natural part of life, but in a co-parenting relationship, they often carry deeper emotional weight. New relationships, blended families, remarriage, relocation, and career changes can all reshape the structure of a child's world. These shifts can feel overwhelming for parents who want to protect their child while balancing personal growth, healing, and new chapters in their own lives. Yet these transitions do not have to weaken the co-parenting partnership. With healthy communication, emotional intelligence, and a commitment to placing the child's well-being at the center, new family dynamics can become opportunities for growth, stability, and love.

Two homes can feel like two different worlds for a child. Different routines, different rules, and different parenting styles can easily create confusion or emotional tension. Children thrive on predictability and consistency. They need a safe, loving environment where their feelings are heard, their routines are understood, and their sense of belonging is affirmed. When transitions are handled with care, children learn that change can be navigated peacefully, even when life feels uncertain.

The phrase, "the child in the middle," is more than a description. It is a reminder of how deeply children internalize the emotional atmosphere around them. They do not have the maturity to separate their parents' conflict from their own sense of security. They feel caught in the tension between two worlds when transitions are not handled with sensitivity. My personal reflection about watching my grandchildren navigate difficult transitions speaks to the heartache many parents experience. Wanting to fix everything for the sake of the child is a natural response, but some situations are beyond a single person's control. What remains within reach, however, is the power to model emotional strength, compassion, and spiritual grounding. As a grandmother, one of the hardest things I have ever had to do is watch my grandchildren navigate situations that feel too heavy for their young hearts.

Everything in me wants to step in and fix relationships, mend marriages, restore the households, and strengthen the spiritual foundation I know they need. I want to shield them from disappointment and confusion, verbal abuse, disrespect, humiliation, control, and embarrassment because I understand what instability can do to a child. However, I have learned that while I know I may not be able to fix every broken place, I can be a steady one. I can be a voice of truth, prayer, and consistency. I can model faith when circumstances are shaky and love them when things feel divided. I choose to stand in the gap, praying over their homes, speaking life into their futures and reminding them that God is still at work. I trust, pray and watch.

Children learn by observing. When they see their mother or father treated with respect, even in uncomfortable or disappointing situations, they learn that conflict does not have to destroy relationships. They learn that love can be steady even in seasons of change. They learn that people can disagree without becoming enemies. They learn that family can look different and still be healthy. The modeling of respect becomes a teaching tool that shapes their emotional development for years to come.

Healthy transitions in co-parenting begin with emotional intelligence. This means recognizing your own emotions, understanding the emotions of your co-parent, and responding with clarity rather than impulse. Emotional intelligence also means acknowledging that change can trigger old wounds, insecurities, or fears. A new romantic partner, for example, may stir up questions about belonging or parental influence. A relocation may create concerns about distance, time, or accessibility. A major career shift may impact schedules or availability. These feelings are valid, but they do not have to control the narrative. When parents approach transitions with honesty, empathy, and open communication, they protect the child from feeling the weight of these adult emotions.

Introducing a child to new family dynamics should always be done thoughtfully. Children should not feel rushed into relationships they are not emotionally ready for. A slow and steady introduction helps them adjust without pressure. When both parents communicate respectfully about new relationships, they create a sense of unity and reassurance. Even if the adults are no longer together, the child benefits tremendously from seeing their parents support one another's emotional well-being. It communicates that love is not lost, only transformed. It shows that family bonds can be resilient even through change.

Respect also plays a central role in transition periods. Respecting each parent's household, choices, and personal life honors the partnership you are building for your child. Respect prevents unnecessary conflict, jealousy, or competition between homes. When parents respect each other's decisions, even when they disagree, they create space for mutual trust. Children watch this trust unfold, and it teaches them that stability does not depend on perfection but on cooperation and kindness.

Blended families bring their own complexities. A remarriage introduces new adults, new routines, and sometimes stepsiblings. These changes can be overwhelming for children who are still adjusting to life between two homes. They may feel unsure of their place or wonder how the new dynamics affect their relationship with each biological parent. Clear communication between co-parents helps the child transition smoothly. Setting expectations, explaining roles, and reassuring the child of unconditional love can ease anxiety and build confidence. Coparents can also reassure their child that they are loved unconditionally by both parents, and that their love does not change even though the family structure may be a little different. They can clearly explain their roles and that no one is being replaced. Remind the child that the same routines and traditions exist, and that they can freely ask questions or feel emotional. Lastly, they can let the child know they are working together, and they will not have to choose sides.

Blended-family transitions thrive on unity rather than competition. When new partners support the child's relationship with both biological parents, the child feels safe and valued. When stepparents approach their role with humility, patience, and gentle leadership, children feel respected rather than pressured. A successful blended family does not replace the child's original household structure. It simply expands it with new love, new support, and new opportunities for connection.

Scripture offers powerful guidance when navigating emotionally charged transitions. Colossians 3:13 reminds us to let go of bitterness and release past hurts. Forgiveness is the key that unlocks emotional freedom. It does not mean condoning harmful behavior or forgetting the past. It means releasing the weight of anger so you can move forward with clarity and peace. Forgiveness creates space for God's presence to work within the family. When forgiveness flows, communication becomes gentler, respect grows stronger, and boundaries become easier to maintain.

Additionally, the Biblical Fruits of the Spirit offer a blueprint for creating a peaceful environment during transitions. When a home is filled with the fruits of love, joy, peace, patience, kindness, goodness, faithfulness, gentleness, and self-control, emotional healing begins to manifest. These qualities soften conversations, reduce tension, and influence how children perceive change. A child who lives in a home full of peace learns to move through transitions with confidence. A child who witnesses self-control learns to trust the atmosphere around them. A child surrounded by love learns resilience.

Transitions become more manageable when conversations are simple and focused. Every conversation between co-parents does not need to feel like a battle. Many topics are routine, necessary, and can be addressed with ease. School schedules, extracurricular activities, medical appointments, and everyday decisions should not drain or frustrate either parent. When communication remains calm and consistent, both households function more smoothly. Simple conversations become opportunities to work as a team rather than opponents. Although I know at times certain conversations are not always simple and focused. In these moments, parents can try to redirect the conversation and approach by using a calm tone or break it up into smaller conversations. This technique brings clarity, reassurance, and problem-solving, all while keeping the child's emotional state safe.

Cooperative communication is not about winning. It is about finding common ground that supports the child's well-being. When parents use communication to build rather than destroy, they model maturity and emotional balance. They show their child that conflict can be navigated with grace and that solutions can be found without harming relationships. Cooperation does not erase differences. It simply elevates the child's needs above personal pride.

Emotionally intelligent communication becomes especially important during major life transitions such as relocation or career changes. These shifts require honest discussion, careful planning, and consideration of how the change will affect the child's daily life. Decisions involving relocation should prioritize the child's access to education, healthcare, extended family, and emotional support systems. Career changes may influence parenting schedules or financial responsibilities, and co-parents should approach these changes with understanding rather than accusation. When parents see each other through a lens of compassion, they strengthen the entire family system.

Children benefit most when transitions are handled slowly, thoughtfully, and with intention. They need reassurance that they remain loved and important in both households. They need to know that the adults will continue to show up for them even when circumstances shift. Predictability, open communication, and shared routines can help children feel grounded during seasons of change. Stability does not mean keeping everything the same. It means creating a loving foundation that the child can depend on regardless of transitions.

It is important to acknowledge that transitions do not only affect children. They also affect parents. Adults may experience grief, fear, excitement, uncertainty, or hope as they adjust to new relationships, careers, or family structures. Co-parents must take time to recognize their own emotions and seek support when needed. Healing allows parents to show up more fully for their child. When parents care for their own emotional health, they create space for healthier communication and calmer transitions.

Trust becomes essential during these seasons. Trust is rebuilt through consistency, honesty, and respect. When co-parents follow through on agreements, communicate openly about changes, and avoid actions that create confusion or instability, trust grows naturally. Even in complicated situations, trust can be rebuilt when both parents are committed to growth.

Navigating transitions requires patience and a willingness to learn together. Co-parenting is not about perfection. It is a process, a journey, and a continuous opportunity to show up with love. What matters most is not whether every question is answered perfectly, but whether the child feels seen, supported, and protected. Two homes can create one unified heart for the child when love is the foundation guiding every decision.

Change does not have to divide families. When approached with humility, communication, and God-centered wisdom, transitions can become powerful moments of transformation. Families can learn to adapt together, create new traditions, embrace blended dynamics, and build a stable rhythm that honors the needs of the child.

Through all transitions, the message remains the same. The child must remain at the center. Their stability, emotional health, spiritual growth, and sense of safety are the guiding focus. With respect, boundaries, forgiveness, and the Fruit of the Spirit present in the home, co-parenting partnerships can weather any transition with grace.

Co-parenting is not a destination or a final achievement. It is a journey filled with learning, evolving, and choosing love over conflict. Co-parenting isn't something you get right away; it doesn't come with a manual, and you don't learn everything all at once, but you do get to continuously show up with love and adjust when you need to. When parents honor one another, communicate with intention, and trust God through the transitions, they give the child a gift that lasts a lifetime. They give them the blueprint for healthy relationships, resilience, and emotional security. They show them that change can be navigated with courage and that love can remain steady through every transition.

CHAPTER 7

THE UNINVITED THIRD PARENT

The Weight of Watching

There is a unique kind of heartbreak that comes when you witness a child suffer, not from their own choices, but from the choices of the adults around them. As a grandmother, I have stood on the sidelines more times than I can count, watching the ripple effects of broken communication, unresolved pain, and misaligned priorities between my children and their co-parents. It is a quiet agony, because while my instinct is to protect and fix, there are limits to what I can do when I am not the parent, yet still so deeply affected.

When my grandchildren were between the ages of 3 and 10, I saw the confusion in their eyes when routines were disrupted. I felt their tension when holidays turned into battlegrounds of scheduling and disappointment. I watched their innocent hearts absorb adult emotions far too heavy for them to carry. Their questions came through silence, through pulling away, and by trying to be the peacemaker in a world they didn't choose. These moments stirred something deep in me, a fierce desire to intervene, to step in, and to become the voice of reason where there seemed to be none. I've realized that as the child gets older, so does communication within a co-parenting relationship. It changes when certain circumstances arise, and flexibility doesn't become an option.

Without fully realizing it, I became what I now call "The uninvited third parent." It was never out of pride; instead, it was out of pain. I found myself mediating arguments, setting boundaries, planning schedules, and stepping into conversations that were not mine to have. I slid into the role of protector and peacekeeper, trying to fill in the gaps left by parents who were still growing, still healing, still learning how to navigate parenting. In my heart, I believed I was helping. And truth be told, there were times when my involvement did ease the tension.

But as time went on, I began to see what I had not seen before. Being a grandmother and knowing that children can't take care of themselves, I would automatically see a need and take care of it. For example, if the boys needed a haircut, I would take it upon myself and take them instead of allowing and waiting for the fathers to do it. When school supplies were needed, I didn't give the parents time to purchase them. Instead, I automatically got them. I would also purchase their clothes and anything they needed without asking or involving the parents. The more I stepped in, the more I interfered. Not intentionally, but subtly. I created a dependency where there should have been accountability. I watched the parents lean on me instead of learning to lean on each other. I recognized moments where my presence, although well-meaning, became a wedge instead of a bridge. And the hardest part to acknowledge was this: I was not modeling faith, I was modeling control.

THE CHILD IN THE MIDDLE

When Worry Becomes a Trap

Worry is powerful. It disguises itself as love, as protection, as responsibility, but at its root, worry grows from fear. I stayed up many nights thinking about my grandchildren, afraid of the emotional scars they might carry, wondering if I had failed them by not doing enough, or by doing too much.

Worry whispered lies into my ear. It told me that I had to fix everything. It told me their future depended on my intervention. It told me that if I stepped back, something would go terribly wrong. I felt that a lot of times, I needed to come to the rescue to save my grandchildren from being in the middle of verbal abuse that was going on in the home. I would also call the fathers and talk to them about certain occurrences.

But God began to gently deal with me. In prayer, I heard a question that pierced me deeply, "Do you trust Me more than you trust yourself?"
That question brought truth to light. My worry had become louder than my worship. My fear of what could go wrong began to outweigh my faith in what God could make right. I was wrestling not with the situation, but with surrender. I had to choose between clinging to control or placing everything at the feet of the One who sees what I cannot see.

The Kingdom Shift

My shift didn't happen in one moment. It was a slow unlearning of everything the world teaches about family roles, protection, and involvement. Through the lens of Kingdom knowledge, I began to understand that the most powerful place I could stand was not in the middle of the situation, but in the gap. The spiritual gap. The prayer gap. The wisdom gap. To me, Kingdom knowledge means knowing how God's ways and rules work and using the understanding as guidance for my life and the decisions that I make. Through Kingdom knowledge, I seek to understand principles, morals, and spiritual truth to align with His purpose for my life.

I learned to forgive, although it wasn't overnight or easy; I learned to speak less and pray more. To stop managing and instead begin mentoring. To release my need to control and take on the heart to counsel, but only when asked, and always with grace. I took my pain to the throne room before I tried to take it to the living room. I shifted from reaction to intercession.

And in that shift, I saw fruit. I saw my children stumble, but I also watched them rise. I saw them learn lessons I once tried to teach them. I saw them begin to parent from their own growth, not my guidance. I saw strength develop where I once tried to patch over weakness. It is all coming together at its own pace, and the fruit is still developing. I realized that stepping back was not abandonment. It was obedience. It was trusting God more than I trusted my own instincts.

It was aligning with the Kingdom order instead of the emotional impulse. Because sometimes the greatest act of love is letting God do what only He can do.

Letting Go, Not Giving Up

Letting go does not mean giving up. It means giving things over. To God. To grace. To growth. It means trusting the process, even the parts that hurt.

What I have learned through this journey is that love does not always look like involvement. Sometimes love is silence. Sometimes love is restraint. Sometimes love is choosing to sit back when everything in you is screaming to step in. Sometimes love is allowing a child, your child or your grandchild, to learn through experience because you know the lesson will shape them in ways your intervention never could.

To every grandparent, caregiver, or loved one who feels the weight of watching a family struggle, I want to tell you this: Be present, but not overpowering. Be prayerful, not panicked. Be Kingdom-minded, not control-driven. Your role is not to take over. Your role is to cover. Because the legacy we leave is not built by fighting every battle for our children, but by equipping them to stand in battle themselves, and to know that God stands with them.

The Power of Forgiveness

Forgiveness has been both the hardest and the holiest part of my journey. In quiet moments, I reflected on the chaos I witnessed and tried to mend, such as health issues occurring with my grandchildren and the divorce of their parents. I realized I wasn't only holding onto fear. I was holding onto offense. Offense at how my children were spoken to. Offense at what my grandchildren had to experience. Offense from my own past wounds resurfacing.

I thought I had forgiven. But true forgiveness is deeper than words. It is choosing not to rehearse the hurt. It is releasing the right to be right. It is laying down anger even when the anger feels justified. It is a blessing that those who wounded you by how they treated someone you love.

I had to forgive both parents, for what they said and didn't say, for what they did and didn't do. I had to forgive myself for overstepping, for trying too hard, and for not always knowing when to be still. And I had to model forgiveness for my grandchildren, not through speeches but through my behavior. Because children learn forgiveness not by being told about it, but by watching it lived out. I modeled forgiveness by my grandchildren witnessing me still being respectful & polite, choosing not to retaliate. I would still bless the other co-parent with Father's Day and birthday gifts. I still showed acknowledgement, and I tried not to let anger take control. I continued to treat them respectfully.

Forgiveness does not mean ignoring pain. It means inviting healing into it. It does not excuse behavior, but it stops bitterness from taking root and becoming a generational curse. Kingdom knowledge taught me that unforgiveness keeps us stuck in the very chaos we want so desperately to escape. But forgiveness, radical, God-centered forgiveness, frees everyone involved. It opens the door to wisdom, maturity, restoration, and peace.

I remind myself often to forgive even when they don't apologize. Forgive because forgiveness was freely given to you. Forgive because peace is more important than proving a point. That is the heart of co-parenting with grace. That is the example I want to leave behind.

Resting in God's Hands

I still carry concerns. I still wipe away tears. I still feel my heart tighten when I see my grandchildren go through things that feel unfair. But now I carry these moments differently. I carry them with peace. I carry them with prayer. I carry them with the understanding that my grandchildren are not just in my care, but in God's hands.

And in His hands, they are safest.

That truth gives me rest. That truth allows me to breathe. That truth reminds me that although I am a grandmother with a heart big enough to want to fix it all, I am also a woman learning daily to trust God with what I cannot control.

The greatest support I can offer my family is not intervention. It is intercession. The most powerful way I can support my family is by going to God in prayer on their behalf, and not trying to solve everything myself. It is love without control. It is wisdom without force. It is being present without overpowering. It is modeling faith in a God who sees every tear, hears every prayer, and covers every child in ways no human ever could.

CHAPTER 8

CO-PARENTING ACROSS DISTANCE:

LONG-DISTANCE PARENTING

Co-parenting across distance introduces unique challenges that many families never anticipate when they first imagine raising a child together. When miles separate households, parenting no longer happens in shared kitchens, coordinated school drop-offs, or quick hallway conversations; instead, it unfolds across phone calls, travel plans, calendars, time zones, and intentional moments that must be protected rather than assumed. Distance adds layers of planning, patience, and trust, yet it does not remove the responsibility or privilege of raising a child well. With care, clarity, and commitment, long-distance co-parenting can remain steady, supportive, and deeply rooted in love.

At its best, long-distance parenting works when both parents stay anchored in what matters most: the emotional well-being of the child. Geography may change logistics, but it should never change values, expectations, or the shared understanding that a child deserves stability, safety, and consistency from both households. When parents commit to respectful communication, coordinated planning, and child-centered decision-making, distance becomes a hurdle to manage, not a wedge that divides.

Clear communication becomes the lifeline of long-distance co-parenting. Without proximity, assumptions quickly replace understanding if communication is not intentional. Parents must be willing to speak clearly, listen carefully, and respond thoughtfully, even when emotions are present. This includes sharing school updates, medical information, schedule changes, and important milestones. Shared calendars, updated contact information, and consistent routines help reduce confusion and anxiety for the child. When both parents stay informed and aligned, the child experiences continuity rather than contrast between households.

Technology, when used wisely, can serve as a powerful bridge rather than a barrier. When the connection is predictable, the child learns that distance does not equal absence.

Ways to Use Technology to Serve as a Communication Bridge
- Make regular video calls
- Leave voice messages
- Share photos
- Send good morning messages
- Say a bedtime prayer over the phone

Yet, technology should never become a tool for surveillance, control, or conflict. Children should not feel pressured to express affection on a screen or carry emotional messages between parents. Communication should be age-appropriate, natural, and focused on the relationship, not reporting. A child should never feel responsible for maintaining the bond between adults. That work belongs to the parents.

One of the greatest risks in long-distance co-parenting is allowing adult tension to spill into the child's emotional space. When parents live far apart, misunderstandings can grow quickly, and unresolved conflict can linger longer. It becomes even more critical to keep adult disagreements away from the child. Speaking neutrally about the other parent, avoiding negative commentary, and refusing to place the child in the middle reinforces emotional safety. A child should never feel that loving one parent means betraying the other.

Children are remarkably perceptive. Even when words are withheld, tone, tension, and silence speak loudly. A child who senses division may internalize it as responsibility or blame. They may feel torn between two worlds, unsure of where they belong or how to remain loyal to both parents. This emotional weight is far heavier than any suitcase they carry between homes. Protecting a child from adult conflict is not a courtesy; it is a necessity.

Honesty plays an important role in long-distance parenting, but honesty must always be balanced with wisdom. Children deserve truthful explanations that are appropriate for their age and emotional capacity. They do not need details of adult disagreements, legal complexities, or financial disputes. What they need is reassurance. Reassurance that both parents love them, that the distance is not their fault, and that they are not required to choose sides. When parents explain changes calmly and confidently, children feel steadier, even in uncertain circumstances.

Flexibility is essential in long-distance co-parenting because life rarely unfolds exactly as planned. Travel delays, work demands, school needs, and developmental changes will require adjustments over time. As children grow, their needs, schedules, and preferences evolve. What worked at age five may not work at age 10 or 15, because at age 5, you can give them little rewards and treats, but at age 10, it is more responsibility involved and more consequences. Then, at age 15, there is often more punishment, more direct commands, more negotiation, more choices, more boundaries and more independence. Therefore, parents must be willing to revisit agreements, renegotiate routines, and adapt with maturity rather than rigidity. Flexibility does not mean inconsistency; instead, it means responding thoughtfully to changing realities while maintaining core stability.

When flexibility is approached with a child-centered mindset, it becomes an expression of love rather than inconvenience. A parent who adjusts a schedule to support a school event, extracurricular activity, or emotional need sends a powerful message: you matter more than my comfort. Over time, these moments build trust and demonstrate teamwork, even across distance.

Trust is another cornerstone of long-distance co-parenting. Trust that the other parent is acting in good faith. Trust that the child is being cared for. Trust that love does not diminish with miles. Without trust, communication becomes defensive, and cooperation erodes. While trust may be difficult, especially when relationships have been strained, it remains essential for the child's sense of security. A child who knows their parents respect one another feels safer navigating two households.

Faith often becomes both an anchor and a guide in long-distance parenting. When physical presence is limited, prayer fills the gaps that hands cannot reach. I have learned through experience that miles may separate parents, but they should never separate purpose. When my mom left my dad, I was 8 months old. She decided to allow my grandmother to raise me, while she moved to Connecticut and my dad moved from Alabama to Florida. It was difficult for them to co-parent as they were in two separate states, miles apart. I believe they should have never left the responsibility on my grandmother to take care of me. I still should have been their priority even when the relationship didn't work out. As a child, I believed it was all about their feelings and emotions, and not mine. There was no accountability taken. Therefore, children should never carry the weight of adult distance or division. Instead, they should feel covered by prayer, surrounded by love, and anchored in the assurance that both parents are united in their commitment to their well-being.

Trusting God in the co-parenting journey requires humility and surrender. It means asking for wisdom before responding in frustration, patience when communication feels strained, and grace when plans fall apart. It means choosing peace over pride and cooperation over control. When parents invite God into their decisions, conversations, and compromises, they allow divine guidance to shape their actions rather than emotional reactions.

Love has no limits or borders. It does not depend on proximity or convenience. Love shows up through consistency, integrity, and presence of heart, even when physical presence is limited. A child who experiences this kind of love learns that relationships are not defined by distance but by commitment. They learn that people can be apart yet still connected, still dependable, still united in purpose.

Long-distance co-parenting also offers opportunities for growth and resilience. Children who experience healthy co-parenting across distance often develop strong communication skills, adaptability, and emotional awareness. They learn that love can be expressed in many forms and that stability is created through intention rather than location. When parents model cooperation and respect, children internalize those values and carry them forward into their own relationships.

However, these outcomes are not automatic. They require effort, self-reflection, and accountability from both parents. It requires parents to set aside personal grievances and focus on the shared responsibility of raising a child. It requires remembering that while adult relationships may change, the parenting relationship remains. Distance does not dissolve that responsibility; it magnifies it.

When parents choose unity over conflict and place the child first, the child remains secure, grounded, and loved. Even when households look different, rules vary slightly, or routines are not identical, the underlying message stays the same: you are safe, you are valued, and you are supported by both parents. This consistency becomes the emotional glue that holds the child together across transitions.

Distance may change logistics, but it should never change loyalty. A child should never question whether they are allowed to love both parents fully. Loyalty conflicts damage a child's sense of self and belonging. Parents must actively remove any language or behavior that suggests competition, comparison, or conditional love. Cooperation is not weakness; it is strength in the service of the child.

Allowing God to guide your actions in long-distance co-parenting means trusting that even when circumstances are imperfect, love can still prevail. It means believing that God's grace covers missed moments, misunderstood conversations, and difficult seasons. It means praying not only for your child, but for the other parent as well. Prayer softens hearts, aligns intentions, and restores perspective.

Though you may be separated by miles, you are united in purpose. That purpose is not personal validation, control, or winning. It is raising a child who feels whole, secure, and loved. When parents keep this purpose at the center, decisions become clearer, communication becomes steadier, and conflict loses its power.

Pray that your child is covered by love, guided by faith, and held together by God's grace. Pray for wisdom in moments of uncertainty, patience in moments of frustration, and humility in moments of disagreement. Pray for the strength to choose cooperation when conflict feels easier.

Long-distance co-parenting is not about perfection. It is about intention. It is about showing up consistently, even when it requires sacrifice. It is about choosing the long view, trusting that the seeds you plant today will bear fruit in your child's emotional health tomorrow.

Apart, but together for them.

CHAPTER 9

THROUGH THEIR EYES: THE SILENT HURT

This chapter reflects on the often unspoken emotional journey of children affected by co-parenting and family transitions. It draws upon the power of memory, those vivid, tender, and sometimes heartbreaking moments that reveal how deeply children absorb their surroundings, even when they lack the words to express their feelings. Children may not have the vocabulary to articulate the confusion, fear, frustration, or longing that lives inside them, but their silent stories are written everywhere. They show up in the questions they ask, in the artwork they create, in the behaviors they exhibit, and sometimes in the things they stop saying altogether.

As a grandmother, I have had a front-row seat to some of these moments. I have watched my grandchildren adjust to life between two homes. I have seen the emotional burdens they carry, burdens far too heavy for their small shoulders. I have watched them search for stability in the middle of adult decisions that they did not ask to be part of. Their eyes reveal more than their words. Their behavior speaks louder than their voices. And their silence often carries the weight of a thousand unspoken questions.

These memories are not just mine. They echo the experiences of countless children who quietly adapt, question, hope, and sometimes struggle to understand a world divided by adult choices. When a child is placed in the middle of parents who cannot work together, it creates a silent wound. The wound may not show at first. In the beginning, it looks like small cracks, tears at bedtime, confusion when rules change from one home to the next, or outbursts that no one can quite explain. But over time, these cracks widen. Inconsistent co-parenting reaches far beyond the moment. It shapes how a child sees themselves, how they trust others, and how they step into adulthood.

Scripture reminds us that children are a heritage from the Lord. Parenting is stewardship. And stewardship requires consistency, not perfection, but consistency. Proverbs tells us to train up a child in the way they should go, and when they are old, they will not depart from it. Training is not simply telling. It is modeling, repeating, guiding, and building through unity. When parents fall short of this, the diminishing effects reach into emotional, spiritual, and relational areas of a child's life.

This chapter explores those effects. It blends personal memories, child development research, biblical wisdom, and the quiet truths children carry inside them. It is a space that honors their unspoken experiences and invites every parent and caregiver to pause long enough to see life through a child's eyes.

Early Childhood: The Foundation of Safety

The earliest years of a child's life are built on trust. Psychologist Erik Erikson described early childhood as a period where a child wrestles with trust versus mistrust. Their entire sense of safety develops from the consistency of care they receive. When parenting is stable, routines are predictable, and love shows up the same way, a child learns that the world is safe and that the people caring for them can be trusted. But when parenting is inconsistent, fractured, or unpredictable, the child learns the opposite. They learn that safety is conditional. They learn that love may or may not last. They learn that their environment can shift at any moment.

Imagine a little girl who lives weekdays with her mother. At her mother's home, bedtime routines include prayers, stories, and structure. On weekends, she goes to her father's home, where bedtime has no routine, rules shift daily, and expectations are unclear. At four years old, she is being taught two versions of safety.

At preschool, she has been throwing temper tantrums. But her tantrums are not misbehavior. They are confusion. She does not understand why rules matter in one environment but are optional in another. Her teachers may label her behavior as problematic, but the root is inconsistency.

Even Scripture presents the danger of divided parenting. The story of Isaac and Rebekah shows that when affection and discipline are inconsistent between parents, children learn patterns of deception, manipulation, or insecurity. What they cannot express in words, they express in behavior.

Research confirms this. Studies show that inconsistent parenting in early childhood leads to heightened anxiety, emotional instability, and difficulty self-regulating. Also, research shows that harsh and inconsistent parental discipline is associated with altered cortical development in children (i.e., Whittle et al., 2022). Children who move between inconsistent homes often feel responsible for managing the emotional climate themselves. Their bodies carry stress long before their minds understand it.

Adolescence: When Instability Grows Louder

Adolescence magnifies everything. Teenagers test boundaries, question authority, and explore identity. When parenting consistency is fractured, adolescents experience instability at a deeper level. They do not just wonder if they are safe; they begin to wonder who they are.

Consider a teenage boy whose parents disagree on boundaries. His father enforces curfews, homework time, and respect. His mother dismisses these rules, allowing anything to go. This inconsistency gives the teen power he is not ready for. He quickly learns how to play one parent against the other. Within months, he is skipping classes, drifting into risky behaviors, and experimenting with substances. His actions are not simply rebellion. They are symptoms of confusion, conflict, and a lack of unified guidance.

Research in adolescent psychology reveals that inconsistent parenting dramatically increases the likelihood of risky behavior, academic struggles, and peer-related issues (i.e., see Halgunseth et al., 2013). When structure collapses, teens build their own rules, and those rules often endanger them.

The Bible speaks directly to instability. James tells us that a double-minded person is unstable in all their ways. Adolescents raised in double-minded households reflect that instability in their friendships, school performance, and relationships. Without unified parental direction, they become divided within themselves.

Adulthood: When Childhood Patterns Become Adult Struggles

Children eventually grow into adults, but the wounds formed in childhood do not disappear at graduation. They show up again and again. They show up in relationships, careers, marriages, and even in how adults parent their own children.

Imagine a young woman raised between two completely different households. One home is strict and emotionally cold. The other is permissive but unpredictable. She grows into adulthood, unsure of how to trust. Her romantic relationships swing between clinging and withdrawing. At work, she struggles with authority because she never learned that rules could be stable and fair. She is successful but exhausted. She has learned to survive, not thrive.

Research on adverse childhood experiences shows that inconsistent parenting increases adult risks of depression, anxiety, trust issues, and chronic stress (i.e., see Felitti et al., 1998). Family systems theory explains that unresolved conflict in one generation often becomes emotional inheritance for the next. Children repeat what they witnessed unless they intentionally break the cycle.

The Bible shows this pattern clearly. Abraham lied about his relationship with Sarah. His son Isaac repeated the same deception. The pattern continued until someone chose differently. Scripture teaches that generational patterns are real, but so is God's mercy and the ability to break cycles through awareness and intentional change.

Seeing Through Their Eyes: The Silent Messages Children Absorb
Children speak through silence. Through drawings. Through behavior. Through questions asked late at night. Their hearts reveal truth in small moments that adults often overlook.

A child who suddenly stops sharing stories is communicating.
A child who clings more tightly during exchanges is communicating.
A child who acts out when transitioning between homes is communicating.
A child who becomes overly independent too soon is communicating.
None of these behaviors is random. They are reflections of a child trying to make sense of instability.

Sometimes their silent stories show up during holidays. Children often feel torn between parents and fear disappointing one while celebrating with the other. Sometimes it shows up at school when a teacher notices the child daydreaming or emotionally shutting down. Other times, it appears in friendships because the child learned early that people may not stay.

This chapter invites parents to slow down long enough to see those signs. To ask themselves not what is wrong with their child, but what their child is trying to express. When parenting is approached with emotional intelligence, parents become more attuned to tone, timing, triggers, and subtle cues. They learn to speak less from frustration and more from understanding.

Blended Families and New Realities

Blended families can bring beauty and support, but they also create emotional complexities for children. A new stepparent, new siblings, new routines, or a new home can be overwhelming for a child who is already navigating divided spaces. Children often fear being replaced or forgotten. Others may carry guilt about liking one home more than the other.

Healthy communication between co-parents is essential in these moments. Children need reassurance that love does not shrink; it expands. Parents must communicate stability, unity, and respect to make transitions smoother. When adults show emotional maturity, children feel safer adjusting to new dynamics.

The Silent Erosion and the Hope of Healing

The greatest danger of inconsistent co-parenting is not one dramatic moment. It is the slow erosion of emotional security. Like water dripping onto stone, inconsistency wears away confidence and peace. Children learn to anticipate disappointment. They learn to brace themselves for conflict. They learn to overcompensate for weaknesses that are not theirs to carry.

But there is hope. Cycles can be broken. Healing can begin at any stage. Parents who are willing to reflect, adjust, communicate, and collaborate can restore safety. Even separated parents can rebuild unity through intentional decisions.

Scripture offers deep comfort here. Joel promises that God restores years that feel wasted. Jesus teaches that steadfast love can heal even after rebellion. God remains the anchor when everything else shifts.

Closing Reflection: A Call to See Through Their Eyes

Jesus said a house divided cannot stand. Parenting divided by inconsistency creates emotional collapse. But when parents choose unity in discipline, communication, and love, they mirror God's unchanging heart. Children raised in that stability flourish. They grow secure, confident, and grounded.

To the child in the middle, your confusion is real, but so is God's unconditional love.

To the parent, your consistency matters. It's more than a responsibility, and it's not just something you do as a parent. It's a ministry that provides safety, guidance and stability for your child. It is not just a duty. It is a ministry. It is healing. It is love made visible. Your stability becomes the answer to the silent stories your children carry.

Children may not tell us everything they feel. But their hearts speak. Their eyes speak. Their silence speaks. Our job is to listen, respond with compassion, and build a foundation strong enough to support the weight of their unspoken stories.

CHAPTER 10

THE HIDDEN BURDEN:

BATTLING MENTAL ILLNESSES

Parenting is already one of life's greatest challenges. When mental illness or untreated behavioral issues enter the picture, the difficulty multiplies in ways most people cannot see. Co-parenting becomes exhausting, overwhelming, and sometimes emotionally dangerous when one or both parents are weighed down by depression, anxiety, trauma, addiction, personality disorders, or years of unresolved anger. These invisible battles do not simply affect the adults involved. They shape the world of the child in the middle.

For that child, the consequences can be devastating. The struggle is not only about whether parents can agree on school schedules or exchange times. It becomes a question of whether the parents can function in a way that provides love, safety, and stability. Many children grow up learning how to read the emotional temperature of the household before they even learn how to read a book. They adapt, they shrink themselves, they predict, they brace for impact, and sometimes they carry responsibilities that belong to adults who are losing their fight with their own minds.

During a counseling session, a father once said, "I want to be there for my daughter, but sometimes I can barely get out of bed. The depression feels like quicksand." His voice trembled as he admitted this, tears rolling down his face. He was not a bad man. He was a broken man. He loved his daughter deeply, but his emotional pain had become a force stronger than his intentions. This is the reality many children live with: parents who love them but are hindered by internal battles they did not choose.

Sometimes mental illnesses do not announce themselves loudly. They creep in through exhaustion, isolation, irritability, or emotional numbness. Sometimes they roar through addiction, explosive anger, or self-destructive choices.

Children absorb it all. They learn quickly when to stay quiet and when to run. They often learn to soothe their parent's emotions instead of being soothed themselves. This reversal of roles creates wounds that do not go away with age. It affects their self-esteem, their relationships, and the kind of parent they eventually become.

The Roots Beneath the Struggle

Parents do not wake up one morning and choose mental illness. From a Biblical and psychological perspective, most emotional struggles are the result of unhealed wounds, generational trauma, or prolonged spiritual and emotional battles. Trauma that is not processed becomes trauma that is passed down. Pain that is not healed becomes pain that leaks into parenting.

Some parents grew up experiencing abuse, neglect, or abandonment. They carry these childhood scars into adulthood, into relationships, and eventually into their parenting. Others battle substance abuse that began as an attempt to soothe emotional pain. Addiction clouds judgment, fuels instability, and damages trust. Some struggle with personality disorders that make emotional regulation feel impossible. Others battle depression, anxiety, panic, or mood disorders that drain their energy so deeply that parenting feels like carrying a mountain.

There are parents whose anger erupts quickly because they were never taught healthy ways to regulate emotions. Their home life becomes a cycle of yelling, breaking down, apologizing, and repeating the same pattern the next week. Others live with spiritual brokenness, weighed down by unforgiveness, guilt, shame, or feelings of rejection. When the heart is heavy, love has a harder time flowing freely; they have not yet learn how to manage their emotions.

And still, these parents love their children. That is the hidden tragedy. Many of them are fighting internal wars no one can see.

When Mental Illness Collides with Co-Parenting

When mental illness affects one or both parents, co-parenting becomes strained in ways that go far beyond scheduling. Inconsistency becomes the norm. A parent may promise to pick up their child for a weekend visit, but never show up. They may genuinely intend to come, but their mind and emotions are too unstable to carry the commitment. For the child, the disappointment becomes a seed of rejection. They begin to wonder if they are lovable. They begin to question if something is wrong with them.

When emotions are unregulated, the smallest disagreement between co-parents can explode into conflict. What could have been a five-minute conversation becomes an argument that lasts for days. Mental illness magnifies stress, blurs reality, and creates defensiveness. Conversations about school, medicine, discipline, or routine become battlegrounds instead of peaceful discussions.

Sometimes the mentally ill parent becomes neglectful, not because they do not care, but because their mind is overwhelmed. They forget school events. They forget meals. They forget to check homework. The healthy parent becomes overburdened, carrying the emotional and practical load for two people. This imbalance creates resentment, bitterness, and exhaustion. And while the adults wrestle with their struggles, the child absorbs the silent tension, learning that love is unstable and security is fragile.

A mother once confessed to her therapist through tears, "My son doesn't understand why I yell. He thinks I hate him. I don't. But the anger controls me." Her brokenness was spilling onto her child without her realizing it. The child was interpreting her pain as rejection when, in truth, she was drowning inside.

Story 1: The Depressed Parent

Kevin struggled with a major depressive disorder. His world felt gray every day. Simple tasks felt suffocating. Every movement felt heavy. He often missed custody weekends, not because he didn't love his daughter, but because he was emotionally paralyzed. His 7-year-old daughter would sit by the window with her backpack, waiting for the sound of his car. Hours would pass. No call. No explanation. Just silence.

She began to feel unwanted. She began to believe she had done something wrong. She stopped asking about him out loud, but inside, she still longed for him.

Through therapy, medication, and accountability partners from his church, Kevin slowly gained stability. It wasn't instant. It wasn't perfect. He saw how it was making his daughter feel and also how she would look. He saw the disappointment in her silent eyes. So, he began to show up. And that consistency rebuilt his daughter's trust one visit at a time. His healing became her healing.

Story 2: The Addicted Parent

Maria battled alcohol addiction after her divorce. Her pain ran deep, and the alcohol numbed her heartache, but it also stole pieces of her stability. Her teenage son became the adult in the home. He made dinner. He paid the bills when she forgot. He hid her empty bottles before guests visited. He hated the burden, but he also felt responsible for her well-being. That role reversal created a heavy resentment and deep confusion.

After a family intervention and a rehabilitation program, Maria took her first steps toward sobriety. She leaned on her faith community and repeated Philippians 4:13 over and over, believing that Christ would strengthen her. Healing was slow. Sobriety was not linear. Some days she stumbled, but she kept choosing recovery. Her son saw her fighting for herself and for him. That fight softened the resentment and opened the door to reconciliation.

Medical and Spiritual Interventions, Walking Toward Healing

Healing the mind requires courage. Healing the soul requires surrender. Healing the heart requires both. Mental illness and emotional struggles are not simply personal failures or spiritual shortcomings. They are battles that affect the brain, the body, and the spirit. When a parent seeks help, they are not declaring weakness. They are declaring war against the things trying to destroy them.

Therapy becomes a lifeline for many parents. It gives them a space where their pain is not judged, their emotions are not misunderstood, and their trauma is not minimized. In therapy, a parent can unpack years of hurt that were buried under survival. They learn new coping skills. They identify triggers. They begin to understand why certain patterns repeat. Family or group counseling helps repair broken communication and rebuild relationships. Many people can access therapy through their employers through the Employee Assistance Program. Also, some non-profit organizations, churches, and schools offer counseling services.

For some parents, medication is necessary. Depression, bipolar disorder, anxiety disorders, ADHD, and other mental health conditions can affect how the brain functions. Medication helps stabilize mood, regulate thought patterns, and create the mental clarity needed to parent effectively. This is not a lack of faith. This is responsible stewardship. God gave wisdom to doctors, counselors, and medical professionals to help His children heal.

Rehabilitation programs become essential for parents battling addiction. Addiction is not just a physical battle. It is emotional, spiritual, and psychological. Rehab addresses the root cause instead of just the symptoms. It gives parents the tools to rebuild sobriety, restore trust, and reclaim their lives. Many rehabilitation programs can be found through employers, community organizations, or the local library.

Spiritual support is equally important. Prayer invites God into the deepest places of brokenness. It lifts what therapy cannot reach. Deliverance prayer helps parents confront generational strongholds, spiritual oppression, and deep-rooted patterns formed in trauma. Deliverance is not frightening or extreme when it is grounded in Biblical truth. It is simply the process of allowing the Holy Spirit to remove what does not belong. It is opening the door for God to heal the mind and restore the soul.

Church accountability provides a layer of support that many parents desperately need. Mentorship, discipleship, and pastoral counseling offer spiritual guidance and emotional grounding. Scripture becomes an anchor when the mind feels like a battlefield. Second Timothy 1:7 reminds parents that God has given them a sound mind, even when their thoughts tell them otherwise. This is not just a promise. It is identity. Through Christ, mental stability is possible.

Community is part of God's healing design. Parents were never meant to battle their struggles alone. Supportive friends, church members, mentors, and family step in to help carry the weight. They pray, encourage, and hold space for healing. As parents, we should continually seek community engagements and involvement such as fitness classes, churches, book clubs, recreational sports events, or meet-up groups.

If a parent ever becomes overwhelmed to the point of considering suicide, reaching out for immediate help is critical. Suicide is not a sign that the parent wants to die. It is a sign that they want the pain to stop. Seeking help protects the parent's life and the heart of the child who depends on them. The suicide hotline number is 988, and the website is www.988lifeline.org.

The Child's Experience, What They Feel but Rarely Say

Children are more spiritually and emotionally perceptive than many adults realize. They sense emotional instability before they can name it. They feel tension before they understand its cause. They hear the unspoken fears behind their parent's silence.

A child watches their parent collapse into bed and wonders if they caused the exhaustion. They hear yelling and assume they deserve it. They notice broken promises and quietly blame themselves. They internalize what is not explained. They assume what is not communicated. Children make meaning out of silence, and that meaning often wounds them.

This leads to confusion. Children begin to wonder why a parent switches from warm to cold without warning. They wonder why the parent who laughs with them one day shuts down the next. Shame takes root when the child feels embarrassed or responsible for their parent's emotional instability. Fear grows when they worry that their parent may disappear, relapse, or harm themselves. Some children become resentful because they have been forced to grow up too fast.

Biblical psychology teaches that children form their early understanding of love, safety, and identity through the consistency of their parents. When that consistency is disrupted by mental illness or emotional instability, the child's heart becomes divided. Yet children can heal when the adults around them acknowledge their struggles with humility. A simple truth spoken gently can rebuild trust. Words like "Mommy is hurting, and I am getting help" free the child from blame. Honesty combined with action becomes a foundation for healing.

The Crisis Points No One Talks About

There are moments in unhealthy co-parenting situations that become turning points, and these moments are rarely discussed. The moment when a child hears a parent crying in the bathroom and feels helpless. The moment when a child packs their own bag because their parent forgot. The moment when a child sits at school with a stomachache because they are worried if their parent is safe at home. These are silent burdens children carry.

One teenage girl admitted to her therapist, "I didn't want to go to school because I was scared my mom would hurt herself while I was gone." This kind of fear ages a child emotionally by decades. They become hyper-vigilant. They lose their freedom to be carefree. They question what love is supposed to feel like.

A young boy once said, "I thought if I behaved better, my dad wouldn't drink anymore." Children take emotional responsibility that never belonged to them. They try to become healers, fixers, protectors, or emotional shields for their struggling parent. Their spirit becomes burdened. Their joy becomes restricted. Their innocence becomes fractured.

This is why awareness matters. This is why healing matters. The child in the middle sees everything, feels everything, and carries everything, even when they never speak a word.

Overcoming for the Child's Well-Being

Healing begins when a parent acknowledges the struggle. Denial keeps families trapped. Shame keeps healing out. Honesty breaks generational patterns. When a parent can say, "I am struggling, and I want to get better for my child," the atmosphere begins to shift.

Seeking professional help is not a weakness. It is wisdom. Therapy, medication, rehabilitation, pastoral counseling, and recovery programs all work together to help the parent regain stability. The stronger parent may need to establish boundaries to protect the child. Boundaries are not punishment. Boundaries are protection. They ensure the child is not placed in emotional or physical harm.

Children do not need every detail of the parents' struggle, but they do need honest reassurance. They need to hear that the situation is not their fault. They need consistency in routine, affection, discipline, and communication. They need spiritual anchoring through prayer, scripture, worship, and community. When a parent begins to heal, the child begins to breathe again.

A support village becomes vital. Grandparents, aunts, uncles, godparents, teachers, pastors, mentors, and church family can help raise the child during seasons when the parent is healing. God designed community as a shield for the vulnerable, and children benefit when healthy adults step in to fill the gaps.

Biblical Guidance, God's Heart for the Broken
The Bible does not turn away from mental or emotional suffering. It does not silence grief or dismiss overwhelming thoughts. Scripture speaks directly to the mind, the heart, and the places where trauma takes root. God acknowledges the heaviness of human emotions, and He meets people in the very places they feel most ashamed or alone.

Psalm 147:3 tells us that God heals the brokenhearted and binds up their wounds. This is not only spiritual healing. It is emotional healing. It is psychological healing. It is the restoration of the mind, the mending of identity, and the repairing of self-worth. Isaiah 41:10 offers reassurance to the anxious and the overwhelmed, reminding parents not to fear because God is with them. He promises to strengthen them and help them, even on the days when they cannot stop crying or cannot find the strength to get out of bed.

Romans 12:2 speaks directly to mental health. The renewing of the mind is not metaphorical. It is a transformation. God has the power to change thought patterns, to interrupt generational trauma, to stabilize emotions, and to restore clarity where confusion once lived. Biblical psychology teaches that the mind, the soul, and the spirit must all come under God's alignment for true healing to begin. Trauma distorts identity. Anxiety distorts perception. Depression drains hope. Addiction numbs pain. God restores what trauma tried to steal.

Deliverance and inner healing are also part of God's restorative process. Deliverance frees the mind from spiritual oppression and deep-rooted emotional strongholds formed through trauma, rejection, abandonment, and generational patterns. It is not dramatic or frightening when understood correctly. It is a cleansing of the soul. It is the Holy Spirit removing what the enemy planted. It is the moment when a parent finally breathes freely and says, "This will not control me anymore." God desires wholeness not only for the parent, but for the child who depends on that parent's stability.

Mental illness does not disqualify a parent from God's love. Struggle does not make them unworthy. Emotional battles do not make them incapable of healing or parenting. God specializes in taking what is broken and making it whole again. He does not shame the wounded. He calls them closer.

The Hope of Transformation

When a parent seeks healing, the entire family begins to shift. A parent who heals creates a safer emotional environment for their child. A parent who becomes mindful learns to communicate differently. A parent who breaks generational trauma raises a child who will not have to fight the same demons.

Transformation is possible, no matter how dark the past has been. Kevin learned to overcome depression. Maria rebuilt her life after addiction. Countless parents have learned to manage bipolar disorder, anxiety, PTSD, or explosive anger through therapy, medication, prayer, discipline, and community support. Some parents become stronger through their struggles, not weaker.

Healing is rarely linear. There will be setbacks. There will be days of relapse, days of emotional shutdown, days of guilt, and days when the enemy whispers that nothing has changed. But change is happening. Healing is forming. Every counseling session, every prayer, every boundary, every moment of self-awareness, every breath a parent takes before reacting instead of yelling is evidence of transformation.

God honors the effort, not perfection. And a child can feel the difference. When healing enters a home, the atmosphere changes. Peace returns. Stability grows. Communication becomes softer. Trust begins to rebuild. A child who once walked on eggshells begins to relax their shoulders and breathe normally again.

Reflection and Journaling

Healing Starts with You

Healing begins when a parent becomes brave enough to tell themselves the truth. It begins with reflection, introspection, prayer, and self-examination. Journaling is one of the most powerful tools in emotional healing because it allows the heart to speak without interruption. If you have never journaled before, start by writing down one honest sentence that reflects your feelings. I like journaling because no one ever has to read your writing, it will never be proofread, I can say how I feel, whether it is good or bad, and I can be honest. Journaling doesn't require a perfectly structured paragraph or a particular way of writing. In the exercise, you are just releasing whatever you are feeling or any emotions you're having. It allows you to express yourself with no explanation needed to anyone, and the best part about it is that no one will ever have to read it.

You may start by asking yourself if you have noticed any patterns of mental or emotional struggle in your life. Perhaps it has been trauma that remains unhealed, anxiety that overwhelms your thoughts, anger that erupts faster than you intend, addiction that numbs you, or depression that drains your energy. Reflect on how these struggles show up in the way you respond to your child or your co-parent. Consider whether unresolved wounds from your own childhood or relationships are shaping your parenting decisions, expectations, or reactions today.

Ask yourself if you have minimized your struggles, denied them, or excused them instead of seeking help. Consider whether you have placed emotional pressure on your child by expecting them to comfort you, fix you, or stabilize you during moments when you feel overwhelmed. Reflect on the ways your co-parent may have carried extra weight because your struggles were not fully addressed.

Begin shifting your reflection into action. Think about what medical or therapeutic support may help you become a healthier parent. Counseling, therapy, medication, and recovery programs can provide tools that prayer alone cannot. Ask yourself who in your life can be part of your support circle. Is it a trusted pastor, church mentor, counselor, family member, or friend who encourages accountability and growth? Consider how you can introduce more stability for your child even while you are healing.

Spiritually, reflect on which scriptures speak to your heart and your specific struggles. Identify verses that remind you of God's promise to renew your mind and restore your strength. Ask yourself how prayer, worship, or journaling can become consistent parts of your emotional recovery.

Determine where you need to release unforgiveness toward yourself, your co-parent, or others so that God's grace can flow more freely into your parenting and your home.

Reflection is not about condemnation. It is about awareness. Awareness becomes the first chapter of healing.

Closing Thought for Parents

Healing is not about being flawless. It is about being faithful. Every step toward wholeness is a step that blesses your child. Choosing to heal is choosing to break generational cycles, restore hope, and interrupt patterns that have existed for decades. It is choosing to hand your child a future that is not chained to yesterday's pain.

You will not heal perfectly. But you will heal purposefully. And your child will feel the difference in the warmth of your voice, the steadiness of your presence, and the softness of your spirit.

The child in the middle may not understand every detail of your journey, but they will feel your transformation. They will witness the peace return. They will witness the atmosphere shift. They will witness the love grow stronger.

Mental illness is not the end of your story. It is a chapter. Healing is possible. Restoration is real. And God is with you through every tear, every breakthrough, and every moment you choose to rise again.

CHAPTER 11

DOLLARS & SENSE

Money is never just about dollars. It is about sense. The sense of security a child feels knowing their needs will be met. The sense of stability that surrounds them when food is always on the table, clothes fit comfortably, and school supplies are ready at the start of each year. And the sense of love that grows in a child's heart when they recognize that both parents are invested in their future, not only emotionally but also financially. A child may never articulate these feelings in adult terms, but they experience every one of them. They know when their world is stable. They know when they are supported. And they certainly know when something is missing.

Too often in co-parenting, financial support becomes a battleground. One parent gives consistently, while the other is inconsistent, dismissive, or deliberately withholding. Sometimes the absence of financial contribution has nothing to do with inability. It is rooted in resentment, anger, jealousy, or a desire to punish the other parent. But here is the truth every parent must hear: financial contribution is never about supporting the other parent. It is about supporting the child. The money does not belong to the adults. It belongs to the child whose life both parents helped create. When one parent refuses to contribute, the child pays the price, emotionally and materially.

The Emotional Impact of Financial Neglect

Children 13 years old and under often do not understand bank accounts or court orders. They sometimes cannot comprehend child support arrangements or financial disputes. What they do understand is absence. They understand when their needs are met and when they are left waiting. They understand when they watch classmates go on field trips they cannot afford. They understand when their shoes feel tight while one parent drives up in a new vehicle. A child may never say a word, but their heart absorbs the message: you are not worth the investment.

I once heard a story of a mother raising her son alone after the father stopped providing support. The father had a stable job, but justified neglect by saying he did not want to give her money for her own benefit. What he refused to see was that his contribution was never about her. It was about giving his child the dignity of having the same opportunities as his peers. While the father relaxed in comfort, the son sat in classrooms, noticing the differences. He saw other children wearing new shoes at the start of the school year. He watched his friends sign up for sports and activities he could not afford. He carried silent disappointment, not because he wanted luxury, but because he wanted fairness. Lack of financial support became a shadow over his childhood.

When financial neglect occurs, children carry an invisible weight. They witness the stress of the parent who is trying to make ends meet. They overhear conversations they should not hear. They feel the tension in the home when bills pile up or when they sense their parent suffering silently. Some children even begin working earlier than they should, not because they want independence, but because they know their parent needs help. That kind of responsibility belongs to adults, not children. But when one parent withholds support, the child becomes the one caught in the middle, trying to fill the gaps.

Why Parents Withhold Support

Parents withhold financial support for many reasons, but none of them are rooted in love. Resentment leads a parent to say, "Why should I pay when they left me?" Anger leads another to say, "I will show them they can't control me." Jealousy whispers, "They have moved on, so I will keep my money to myself." Control turns into manipulation, saying, "If I do not pay, they will have to come back to me." These motives are rooted in emotional immaturity, not in parental responsibility. If one parent is bearing the burden of providing financially, the strain will eventually affect the child's well-being. Co- parenting can't move forward if financial responsibility isn't shared properly. Addressing this is essential to ensure that stability is considered a long-term goal. The child becomes collateral damage in a war they never chose.

Co-parenting requires emotional intelligence. Emotional intelligence means understanding that co-parenting is not a stage to perform past hurt. It is a call to rise above personal emotions and do what is right for the child. Scripture reminds us in Philippians 2:4 to look beyond our own interests and consider the needs of others. When a parent withholds support to teach the other parent a lesson, the child is the one who suffers. This is not the heart of God, nor is it aligned with responsibility.

Co-parenting is not about reliving yesterday's pain. It is about building tomorrow's stability. You cannot move forward while dragging bitterness behind you. You cannot raise a thriving child while choosing actions rooted in revenge. Love does not withhold. Love provides. Love shows up.

The Kingdom Principle of Provision

In the Kingdom of God, provision is a form of stewardship. God models this as our Father: My God will supply every need of yours according to His riches in glory in Christ Jesus. Children look to their parents the same way. They expect their needs to be met by the people responsible for their lives. When a parent chooses to neglect, they step outside of God's order for family and responsibility.

Jesus spoke strongly against hypocrisy. He called out those who claimed righteousness yet ignored the needs of the vulnerable. A parent cannot claim to love their child while refusing to support their daily life. Financial support is not a favor. It is a covenant responsibility.

Responsibility in co-parenting means partnering with God in nurturing, protecting, and providing. Financial support is one of the ways parents demonstrate that partnership. Whether the household is blended, separated, or transitioning, the child's needs stay consistent. Their meals do not disappear because an adult is angry. Their school supplies do not vanish because their emotions are hurt. Their clothing does not stretch because adults are battling pride. Provision must continue regardless of the emotional landscape.

Maturity in Financial Responsibility

I once heard a father say to his daughter, "I do not have much to give, but you will always know I gave what I had." Those words held more value than money. They carried honor, humility, sacrifice, and love. A child will always remember effort. A child will always recognize consistency. Even when finances are limited, the presence of responsibility teaches the child that they matter deeply.

Being a responsible parent is more than earning money. It is about stepping up, remaining accountable, and giving consistently. Children remember who showed up. They remember who made the effort. They remember who invested in their life. Lack of funds is not the problem. Lack of effort is.

Paul wrote in 1 Corinthians 13:11 that when he grew up, he put away childish things. When a parent withholds support due to anger or jealousy, that is childish behavior. Maturity means leaving behind emotional impulses and choosing responsibility. Maturity means saying, "This child deserves stability no matter how I feel about the other parent." Maturity means acknowledging that the child did not ask for the circumstances that created the co-parenting dynamic, but they still need love and support.

Healing, Accountability, and Rebuilding Trust

For the parent who has failed in this area, redemption is always possible. Healing starts with honesty. It begins with acknowledging the neglect, asking God for forgiveness, and making a commitment to show up consistently going forward. Rebuilding trust is not about making promises. It is about taking action. Children pay attention to consistency more than apologies.

For the parent carrying the financial weight alone, know that God sees your sacrifice. Scripture calls Him a Father to the fatherless, a defender of those abandoned and burdened. When you carry more than your fair share, God carries you. You may feel tired, stretched thin, or unseen, but Heaven sees every meal you provided, every bill you paid, every tear you cried, and every time you held your child together while holding yourself together too.

And for the child, the goal is never to turn them against the absent parent. The goal is to teach responsibility, grace, and accountability. The goal is to model God's order even in brokenness. The goal is to show the child that maturity means showing up even when it is hard.

Dollars and Sense Working Together

Dollars without sense become wasted. Sense without dollars creates strain. But when both come together, a child experiences emotional and financial balance. They learn that they are worth the investment. They learn that love is more than words. They learn that stability is possible in two homes. They learn that parents can rise above conflict for their sake.

Parents must remember that financial support is not a gift. It is not charity. It is not leverage. It is not ammunition. It is a covenant responsibility to the child God entrusted to you. Withholding support because of pride or hurt is choosing emotional immaturity. Giving consistently, even when relationships change, is choosing God's Kingdom way.

When both parents practice responsibility, communication, emotional intelligence, and respect, the child in the middle grows up with confidence rather than confusion, trust rather than fear, and stability rather than struggle. When you practice responsibility, it requires you to prioritize the child's needs and not personal conflict or emotions. Parents must ensure that children have stable routines for events such as mealtime and homework sessions. This sense of normalcy is created through effective and concise communication. Co-parenting requires many things, but at the heart of it is love expressed through action. And that love must include provision.

Children deserve a childhood filled with security, not suffering. They deserve stability, not scarcity. They deserve parents who give not out of obligation, but out of love.

Dollars create opportunities. Sense creates peace. Together, they create a foundation strong enough to support the child in the middle and help them flourish into who God designed them to be.

CHAPTER 12

SELF-CARE: MAINTAINING YOUR WELL-BEING

Co-parenting can be emotional, especially when there are unresolved conflicts, disappointments, or unspoken wounds that linger beneath the surface. Emotional support and self-care are essential pillars in building a successful co-parenting foundation. Navigating shared parenting responsibilities can be demanding, draining, and overwhelming at times, particularly when past relationships still speak loudly in your heart. Taking time to care for yourself mentally, emotionally, and physically strengthens your ability to parent with wisdom and clarity. It also models healthier behaviors for your child or children. A co-parent who feels grounded and supported is better equipped to make thoughtful decisions, communicate with intention, and provide a stable environment. When you pour into yourself, you strengthen everything connected to you, including the child in the middle.

Additionally, co-parenting challenges take a toll on the mind and spirit, but caring for yourself creates space for healing. Taking time for yourself does not mean being selfish. It means honoring your emotional well-being so you can show up as the parent your child deserves. Eating well helps your body stay nourished, so you do not feel like you are going through. Moving your body gives you energy, so you do not look like what you are going through. Prayer renews your spirit and shifts your focus away from the wrong things. Romans 12:2 reminds us that God renews our mind and our soul. That renewal is essential when you are working through the complexities of co-parenting.

When I look back and think about myself at 18, raising twins before I even had time to discover who I was, I realize how much emotional support I needed. At that age, I was trying to figure out how we were going to take care of two babies while we were practically still babies ourselves. My version of self-care at that time was completely surface-level. I was mostly concerned with getting my pre-baby body back. I weighed 118 pounds before pregnancy, and I didn't want to look like I was falling apart. I didn't want to look like what I was going through. I wanted to look strong even when I felt lost. But true self-care goes deeper. It is not just about how you look. It is about nurturing your emotional and spiritual health as much as your physical appearance. The glow that comes from peace is a different kind of glow. It comes from within.

Creating a Support Network

You are not meant to walk this co-parenting journey alone. One of the greatest gifts you can give yourself is a circle of people who care about your healing and your growth. Support can come from family, friends, mentors, spiritual leaders, or professional counselors. Sometimes simply talking through your thoughts with someone who listens without judgment can bring clarity and peace. Connection reminds you that you are not the only person navigating these emotional storms.

Look for opportunities to connect with others who understand the complexity of co-parenting. This may be a parenting group at your church, a local meetup group, or even an online Facebook/social media group that can assist you in finding trusted individuals who can encourage you. Many parents find comfort in support groups where they can share their stories, vent their frustrations, and receive encouragement. Isolation makes struggles feel heavier. Community lightens the load. Scripture tells us to bear one another's burdens because mutual support is part of God's design. Just knowing someone else has been where you are can help you feel grounded.

Professional help is also a powerful resource. Sitting with a therapist or counselor gives you space to unpack emotions that you may not feel comfortable sharing anywhere else. Therapy is not a sign of failure. It is maintenance for the mind and spirit. A therapist who understands family dynamics can equip you with the tools needed to process stress, heartbreak, grief, and emotional trauma. There is strength in seeking help. You do not have to process everything on your own.

The Power of Self-Care

The phrase you cannot pour from an empty cup is more than a reminder. It is a truth that every parent must embrace. Self-care is not indulgence. It is preservation. When you care for your own needs, you give your children a healthier, calmer, and more present version of yourself.

Children feel our stress even when we think we are hiding it. They absorb our energy long before they understand our words. When you model rest, prayer, balance, and self-respect, you teach your child to value those same things for themselves.

A parent who is emotionally nourished creates a peaceful home. A parent who practices self-control and emotional awareness gives the child a sense of grounding. When you are calm, they can breathe. When you are centered, they feel safe. When you are patient, they learn patience. A peaceful parent builds a peaceful home. Self-care gives you that peace. Self-care can be simple, but its impact is powerful. Making time for yourself every day, even if it is only a few minutes of quiet, can help you reconnect with your thoughts and emotions. Listening to worship music, sitting in silence, taking a walk, praying, or simply stepping outside for fresh air can reset your spirit. Jesus Himself withdrew from the crowd to rest and pray, proving that solitude is not weakness. It is spiritual strategy.

Eating well fuels your body so that you can handle the emotional weight of co-parenting. Movement helps release tension that builds up in your muscles and your heart. Rest restores clarity. Prayer resets the mind. Journaling gives your emotions a safe place to land. Connecting with uplifting people helps you remember your strength. Setting boundaries around toxic communication protects your peace. Asking for help prevents burnout. Rediscovering your hobbies helps reconnect you with the joyful parts of yourself that existed long before parenting challenges began. That means taking time out for yourself, prioritizing your personal well-being by exercising, reading, journaling, having a spa day, getting a facial or pedicure, enjoying a mini staycation, walking in the park, or visiting the hair salon or barbershop.

Self-care is a layered experience. It touches your body, your mind, your spirit, your emotions, and your relationships. Every layer matters because every layer influences how you show up as a parent.

Recognizing Burnout

Parental burnout is real, and it creeps in quietly. It begins with exhaustion, then irritability, emotional numbness, zoning out at times, withdrawing from children, difficulty making decisions, having an inability to focus, having unhealthy habits, experiencing loss of appetite, and eventually, finding yourself functioning on autopilot. Burnout steals your joy, your patience, and your clarity. It makes even simple tasks feel overwhelming. If you feel consistently drained or disconnected, pause. Take an honest inventory of your emotional health. Ask yourself what you need. Consider where you have been neglecting your self-care. Reach out for help. There is no shame in needing support. Self-care is not avoiding your responsibilities. It is strengthening yourself so you can carry them without breaking.

A Personal Testimony of Growth

I did not always understand how to care for myself the right way. At 18, my identity was wrapped up in how I looked after pregnancy, how quickly I could bounce back, and whether the outside world believed I was okay. But I was not okay. I was tired, overwhelmed, and scared. I didn't have the emotional tools I needed. I didn't know what healing looked like. It took years of experience, prayer, counseling, and reflection to understand that true self-care is peace. It is rest. It is allowing yourself to be human, to break, to heal, and to rebuild.

I began to sit with uncomfortable truths instead of running from them. It looked like learning how to pause, breathe and respond instead of reacting. It looked like choosing peace over chaos. I gained these tools by showing up. It wasn't easy to be counseled when it was hard, to pray when I didn't have the answers, and learning that self-care isn't selfish; it was necessary. I had to learn how to give myself grace and how to start over without shame. The tools also came from patience in knowing that consistency was the key and believing that rebuilding didn't mean that I failed. Instead, it meant now that I had gained the wisdom to grow. The young woman I was back then didn't know what she needed. But I thank God I kept growing.

If you are a parent reading this and you feel tired, stretched thin, or emotionally worn, hear me clearly. It is okay to start over. It is okay to change your routine. It is okay to ask for help. You do not have to have it all figured out. Healing takes time. Growth requires grace. Just begin with one small act of self-care. Choose one thing that brings peace to your spirit and practice it consistently. Your peace matters. Your healing matters. You matter.

Faith and Emotional Resilience

The Bible is full of wisdom for emotional renewal. It teaches gratitude, forgiveness, humility, patience, and grace. These are not just spiritual principles. They are emotional strategies that help you stay grounded when life becomes overwhelming. Letting go of bitterness frees your heart. Forgiving those who hurt you shifts the spiritual atmosphere. Practicing gratitude re-centers your mind. Receiving God's grace strengthens your spirit. Healing is not instant, but it is always possible when you remain open to growth.

Romans 12:18 teaches us that peace is a partnership. It says, if it is possible, as far as it depends on you, live at peace with everyone. Do what you can. Control your part. Release the rest to God. When you do your part, God meets you where you are and helps you with the rest.

Matthew 11:28 invites us to come to Jesus when we are weary, burdened, and tired of holding everything together. That invitation still stands. God offers rest for your soul, comfort for your tears, clarity for your confusion, and strength for your journey.

Faith is not separate from emotional resilience. It is woven into it. When prayer becomes part of your emotional care, peace becomes part of your life. When scripture becomes part of your daily reflection, strength becomes part of your identity. When forgiveness becomes part of your growth, freedom becomes part of your future.

Emotional support and self-care are not luxuries. They are necessities. Your well-being is not separate from your parenting. It is the foundation of it. The stronger, healthier, and more grounded you are, the more you can offer your child. Co-parenting requires patience, emotional maturity, and spiritual grounding. You deserve support while carrying all of that.

Take this chapter as your reminder that you matter. Your healing matters. Your growth matters. Your peace matters. Every step you take toward caring for yourself is a step toward creating a healthier environment for the child in the middle. When you thrive, your child thrives. When you heal, your child learns what healing looks like. When you stand strong, your child learns resilience.

Isaiah 40:31 promises that those who hope in the Lord will renew their strength. Let that strength carry you forward into peace, into joy, into grace, and into the next version of yourself. You deserve it. Your children deserve it. And the journey is worth it.

Everyday Self-Care for Co-Parents

Self-care is not selfish. It is strength. When you take care of your mind, body, and spirit, you become a calmer, more patient, more resilient parent. These everyday practices are simple, powerful, and spiritually aligned steps that help you refuel so you can continue pouring into the child in the middle with grace.

1. **Time to Yourself**

   Make it a daily practice to spend even 10 to 15 minutes doing something that feeds your soul. Sit in silence. Listen to worship music. Take a slow walk. Sip tea on the porch. Jesus Himself withdrew from the crowds to be alone and pray, as seen in Luke

5:16. His example reminds us that solitude, reflection, and rest are not signs of weakness but essential ingredients for renewal.

2. **Healthy Eating**

   Nourish your body so your mind can stay clear and balanced. When you eat well, you feel better physically, mentally, and emotionally. Avoid skipping meals and living on fast food. Make time for foods that fuel your body rather than drain it. Scripture reminds us in 3 John 1:2 that the health of our body and soul is connected. Honor both.

3. **Movement and Exercise**

   You do not need to be a fitness expert to care for your body. Take a walk around the block. Stretch for a few minutes. Dance in the kitchen with your children. Movement relieves stress and lifts your spirit. It is not about appearance. It is about joy, energy, and honoring the temple God has given you.

4. **Rest as a Priority**

   Sleep is not a luxury. It is a necessity. Release guilt about resting. Even God rested on the seventh day. Psalm 127:2 reminds us that He gives His beloved sleep. You do not have to push yourself to the point of exhaustion to prove your worth. Rest is holy. Rest is healing. Rest is part of the journey.

5. **Prayer and Renewing the Mind**

   Prayer is oxygen for the soul. When you feel overwhelmed, confused, or tired, take your concerns to God. You do not need polished words. Just honesty. Romans 12:2 teaches that our minds are renewed when we connect with God. Prayer resets the heart, shifts your perspective, and makes room for God's peace.

6. **Journaling and Emotional Expression**

   Give your emotions a safe place to land. Writing helps bring clarity, release stress, and process what words cannot always express out loud. Use your journal to talk to God, to work through your fears, or to celebrate small victories. Include gratitude daily. Gratitude softens the heart and transforms the mind.

7. **Uplifting Social Connections**

   Spend time with people who strengthen your spirit. Surround yourself with family, friends, and church community members who speak life into you. Ask for help when you need it. Let someone babysit so you can rest. You were never meant to do life alone. God places people in our path to support us.

8. **Boundaries as Self-Respect**

   Setting boundaries is a form of emotional maturity. You can limit conversations that are draining or destructive. You can choose when to respond and how to respond. You do not have to be available for conflict at all times. Boundaries are not barriers to connection; they are gates that protect your peace.

9. **Delegate When You Can**

   Let others help you. You do not have to carry every responsibility yourself. Delegating does not diminish your strength. It shows wisdom and humility. Allowing others to assist you gives you time to breathe, heal, and recharge.

10. **Rediscover Joy Through Hobbies**

    You are more than your title, your responsibilities, or your struggles. Reconnect with the things that make you smile. Paint. Cook. Sing. Garden. Play a sport. Laugh often. Proverbs 17:22 says that a cheerful heart is good medicine. Joy is a spiritual strategy. Make space for it intentionally.

CHAPTER 13

CO-PARENTING SUCCESS:

RAISING HAPPY RESILIENT CHILDREN

Co-parenting success is not measured by the absence of conflict or the ability of adults to agree on every issue. True success is reflected in the emotional well-being of the child. Children do not need perfect parents or identical households. They need safety, stability, and freedom from adult burdens.

This chapter serves as both reflection and resolution, an invitation to move forward intentionally, grounded in the understanding that children thrive when adults prioritize their peace over personal conflict. The work of co-parenting does not end with separation. In many ways, it begins there.

Success in co-parenting is often misunderstood. Many parents believe it requires harmony, shared opinions, or equal parenting styles. In reality, successful co-parenting is outcome-focused. It is defined by whether a child feels secure, emotionally supported, and free to love both parents without guilt or fear.

Children raised in healthy co-parenting environments tend to demonstrate emotional regulation, confidence, adaptability, and trust in relationships. These outcomes are not the result of parental agreement, but of intentional choices that protect the child's emotional world. Co-parenting success centers on the child's experience, not the parents' differences.

Emotional safety is the cornerstone of resilience. A child who feels emotionally safe knows their feelings matter, their voice is heard, and their emotional expression will not result in punishment, withdrawal, or conflict.

When emotional safety exists, children develop coping skills and emotional intelligence. When it is absent, children may internalize anxiety, assume responsibility for adult emotions, or suppress their own needs to maintain peace.

Parents must regularly reflect on whether their words, tone, and actions create a sense of calm or tension for the child. Divorce or separation alone does not harm children. Ongoing emotional instability does.

One of the most harmful patterns in co-parenting is placing children in adult roles, particularly as messengers between parents. When children are asked to relay information, negotiate schedules, or carry emotional messages, they become emotionally burdened and experience loyalty conflicts.

Healthy co-parenting requires adult-to-adult communication. Children should never be responsible for managing adult logistics, emotions, or disputes. Removing the child from this role allows them to reclaim their childhood and reduces unnecessary emotional stress.

Children do not require identical rules or routines across households. They require predictability. Consistency provides security, while control often fuels conflict.

Consistency includes reliable schedules, clear expectations, emotional steadiness, and reassurance during transitions. Attempts to control the other household often create power struggles that children feel but cannot resolve. When parents focus on anchoring the child rather than monitoring one another, children learn adaptability without fear.

Resilience is learned through observation. Children watch how adults respond to stress, disappointment, and conflict. They learn emotional regulation, communication skills, and problem-solving by example.

Resilience is not emotional toughness. It is flexibility, recovery, and the ability to move forward with confidence after challenges. Parents who model calm responses, accountability, and healthy coping equip their children with lifelong skills. Perfection is not required. Intentionality is.

Mistakes are inevitable in parenting. What determines long-term impact is whether repair occurs. Repair teaches children that relationships can recover, accountability matters, and love is not withdrawn during conflict.

Sincere repair includes acknowledging wrongdoing, apologizing without justification, and committing to improved behavior. These moments help children understand that conflict does not equal abandonment and that humility strengthens relationships. Repair transforms missteps into learning moments.

Children are individuals with independent emotional experiences. Healthy co-parenting respects their right to feel joy, sadness, and connection in both homes without pressure or guilt.
Children should never feel responsible for protecting a parent's emotions or justifying their affection for the other parent. Love is not finite. When children are free to love openly, their emotional health strengthens.

Boundaries in co-parenting are protective, not punitive. They exist to shield children from adult conflict and emotional overload.

Healthy boundaries include limiting discussions to child-centered topics, maintaining respectful communication, honoring schedules, and keeping disputes private. These boundaries create stability and clarity, allowing children to focus on their own growth rather than adult tension.

Boundaries function as guardrails that support emotional safety.
Successful co-parenting requires a shift from personal grievances to child-focused priorities. A child-centered mindset asks what best

supports the child's emotional well-being, reduces confusion, and models healthy relationships.

This approach does not erase past pain or disagreement. It reframes decision-making around the child's needs rather than adult ego. When parents choose wisdom over winning, children benefit.

Children raised in emotionally safe co-parenting environments often become adults who trust relationships, communicate effectively, and manage conflict with confidence. They learn that love can remain stable even when family structures change.

Even when mistakes have been made, change remains possible. Children are resilient when provided honesty, consistency, and care.

Every intentional decision contributes to a healthier future.
Parents are not defined by separation, but by their response to it. Every choice that protects a child's emotional well-being matters.

Children do not require flawless parenting. They require presence, stability, and freedom from adult conflict. Co-parenting success is not about perfection. It is about choosing the child repeatedly and deliberately.

Children were never meant to manage adult emotions, resolve conflict, or choose sides. They deserve peace, safety, and the freedom to be children. They are seen. They matter. Their well-being is worth protecting.

Children ask for very little: emotional safety, love, and consistency. When adults commit to these principles, children flourish. When children flourish, families heal across generations.

If there's one thing I want you to leave with, it's this: Healing is hard. It's uncomfortable, and it will demand everything from you, but it will change your life if you let it. Growth doesn't come from avoiding the pain; instead, it comes from facing it, learning from it, and refusing to stay stuck in it. I am not here because I was strong; I'm here because I chose myself when it would've been easier to give up. I was broken, I prayed, I rebuilt, I showed up, and I kept going. Every tool I carried, I earned it through acceptance, honesty, accountability, and patience. I had to sit with myself when there was nowhere left for me to hide.

If you're in the middle of this process, don't rush, and don't minimize it. Let it hurt, let it teach you, let it change you. You're not failing if you feel alone. You are becoming what's being built in you right now, and it will carry you for the rest of your life. This chapter marks not only the conclusion of this book but the beginning of a new legacy, grounded in intention, compassion, and responsibility.

When children are protected, they grow strong.
When they grow strong, futures change.
— Deloris Calhoun-Wright

THE CHILD IN THE MIDDLE

PRAYER

This prayer is meant to be used as a moment of pause and surrender, for the parent who is carrying more than they let on. This prayer can also be a prayer of acknowledgement, coming before God honestly. This prayer can be an invitation for healing to ask God to restore what has been strained or feels fragile. This prayer is for covering your child's heart in times and moments of uncertainty, trusting that God will guide you and fix what you can't on your own. Ask God to protect you and your child on this journey.

Heavenly Father,
You are the God who never changes. You are steady, faithful, and true. Lord, I confess that I have not always been consistent in my parenting. At times, I have been distracted, divided, or uncertain. Please forgive me. Help me to walk in unity, patience, and wisdom, so that my child will know the security of Your love through me.

Heal the places where my child has felt confusion or hurt because of inconsistency. Restore what has been broken and protect their heart from carrying these wounds into adulthood. Teach me to parent with love that is firm but gentle, consistent but gracious, reflecting Your own perfect example.

I declare that the cycle of instability stops with me. By Your grace, my child will not inherit the confusion of divided parenting but the peace of a God-centered home. Thank You, Lord, for being my anchor and my child's refuge.

REFLECTIONS & INSPIRATIONS FOR THE

ROAD AHEAD

Keeping the Child at the Heart of Co-Parenting

When parents lead with care and cooperation, *the child in the middle always wins.*

A Legacy of Love and Resilience

A child who feels prioritized and supported carries the lessons of love and resilience for a lifetime.

Putting the Child First

Love shapes a lifetime.

Love First, Always

For *the child in the middle.*

God's Guidance

God's presence goes before me, preparing the path I cannot see yet.

Daily Intention

Each day, choose calm over chaos and growth over bitterness.

AFFIRMATIONS FOR THE JOURNEY

1. I choose peace over conflict, even on the most challenging days.

2. My child feels loved, even when our situation feels complicated.

3. Healing begins with one small act of understanding.

4. I am learning, growing, and becoming a better parent every day.

5. Love is bigger than any disagreement.

6. I release what I cannot control and focus on what I can, which is my heart, my choices, and my peace.

7. My family may not look traditional, but it is whole, strong, and filled with purpose.

8. Every step toward cooperation is a step toward my child's peace.

9. I give myself grace. Parenting through challenges is still parenting with love.

10. My child will not be defined by my struggles. They will rise because of my strength.

THE CHILD IN THE MIDDLE

Made in the USA
Columbia, SC
10 April 2026